T0375173

DEBUNKING DARWINIAN EVOLUTION, GLOBAL WARMING & OTHER MISCONCEPTIONS

WILLIAM C. CEKAL, BSME

Truth concerning unconfirmed
hypotheses that are being perpetuated
as factual and how the scientific
method is being abused

WESTBOW
PRESS®
A DIVISION OF THOMAS NELSON
& ZONDERVAN

WestBow Press books may be ordered through booksellers or by contacting:

WestBow Press
A Division of Thomas Nelson & Zondervan
1663 Liberty Drive
Bloomington, IN 47403
www.westbowpress.com
1 (866) 928-1240

ISBN: 978-1-9736-9265-2 (sc)
ISBN: 978-1-9736-9266-9 (hc)
ISBN: 978-1-9736-9264-5 (e)

Library of Congress Control Number: 2020909545

Print information available on the last page.

WestBow Press rev. date: 07/14/2020

CONTENTS

PREFACE

E verywhere you look today there is talk of evolution, global warming, the "Big Bang" and the expanding universe, alien life and extraterrestrial visitation within our solar system, bigfoot sightings, and other unconfirmed phenomenon. With the advent of immediate global communications, these unconfirmed beliefs are being disseminated worldwide by the media, pseudo-scientists, ill-informed educators, politicians, and those with an unsubstantiated opinion with little or no basis in scientific fact. Nearly everyone believes whatever they are told by the media, politicians, educators or scientists regarding these topics without ever questioning their legitimacy or doing any research on the subject on their own before arriving at a conclusion. All this hype is further enhanced by the majority of the media that takes everything for granted without ever questioning its validity. Most anything that will improve their ratings and will bring in more money is accepted as fact without question. Today, there are numerous television serials and programs that portray these things as truthful without ever informing the viewing public that there are no credible data to back up these outrageous claims. The public is further duped into believing that these programs portray reality by our advanced computer simulations that appear real and have advanced by leaps and bounds from just a few years ago. Now a computer simulation can make believe that the scientific community can obtain significant information from what in reality may be no more than a single pixel of real data. It can be made to look very real and convincing on the TV screen and the public is deceived into believing that it is true.

Pseudoscience is an erroneous belief in theories, hypotheses and assumptions not based on the scientific method. For instance, the almost universal belief in Darwinian evolution is now being taught in schools as actuality, when in fact, it is no more than a poorly researched theory. It is hard to say why these pseudo-scientists are so adamant in basing everything in our Universe on evolution and teaching it in our schools when there are so many obvious reasons why evolution is highly improbable, if not downright impossible. If this trend continues unabated, in a few generations, it will not be questioned by anyone, and they will have obtained their goal of brainwashing the public into their erroneous way of thinking without scientific proof. What is their goal? If evolution is a fact and life was not created through intelligent design, there is no need to have morals and there is no right or wrong. Everyone is free to murder anyone else that does not believe as they do. It justifies rape and other acts of lust, war and genocide since the full title of Charles Darwin's book is "On the Origin of Species by Means of Natural Selection, or the Preservation of Favoured Races in the Struggle for Life". This is part of the basis for Hitler's justification for extermination of the Jews and his quest for world denomination during World War II. Why does anyone need morals if there is no one to answer to for one's behavior and when one's life on Earth is over there is nothing to look forward to except complete and total nonexistence?

There is a belief being perpetuated by politicians, the media and environmental extremists that the Earth is extremely fragile and being destroyed by the actions of man (anthropogenic global warming), when in fact the Earth's surface is massive in relation to regions under human control, is extremely robust and is not subject to the magnitude of changes through man's actions proposed by these radical predictors of impending disaster.

This book has been written in the hope that it will encourage others to examine more fully what they are being led to believe by these pseudo-scientists, politicians, educators and the media. It is hoped that they will question these hypotheses that do not appear to have any real basis in fact and not accept them without question just because they consider their sources to be reliable. Today, there is way too much theoretical nonsense that is being passed off as truth by those that think just because they believe it, it must be true even though they don't have a shred of evidence to support their ridiculous claims. Many of the theoretical scientists that think up some of these foolhardy ideas regrettably do not have any engineering background or concept of just how impractical or downright impossible it would be to incorporate their theories into a practical working solution. Additionally, most of their uninformed audiences are not acquainted with the problems inherent in their suggested incorrect or unproven hypotheses and; therefore, accept these irrational propositions as workable when in fact in many instances they are not.

Many people that write books or articles that reject the "Big Bang" theory, Darwinian evolution or other mistaken beliefs do so for religious reasons. They attempt to prove their beliefs based on teachings from books such as the Bible or Quran, or from the words of various prophets that they hold in esteem. One cannot prove a religious belief to be scientifically correct by referring to something that was said by a highly esteemed theologian. The problem with this approach is that the ones they are trying to convince don't hold their beliefs in such high regard and they believe that science alone holds all the answers. This book does not try to influence anyone as to the validity of any religious values, but instead tries to show why these so called scientific beliefs are not based on reality and do not offer a better explanation than historical records. This book provides numerous scientifically based data in an attempt to discredit these unscientific opinions. The majority of publications that attempt to disprove these erroneous beliefs rely on only one or at most a few scientific parameters to collaborate their rebuttal while this treatise provides extensive factual scientific disclosure on each point of contention for a more comprehensive counter-defense.

Unlike those that deal with practical or applied subject matter, a theoretical scientist usually is concerned with scientific hypotheses and abstract mathematics. The foremost categories of scientists that this book is concerned with are the theoretical disciplines that spend considerable time in the laboratory attempting to understand scientific principles and refine existing theories. These include the Theoretical Physicist, Astrophysicist, Theoretical Biologist, Cosmologist, Evolutionary Biologist, and Theoretical Mathematician as well as numerous others. These scientists usually have an advanced doctorate degree in a theoretical branch of science, often accompanied by a high (genius) IQ, and primarily deal with abstract concepts and assumptions with little regard for their validity or application to realistic circumstances. Most do not conduct testing or experimentation to authenticate their theories, but focus on creating scientifically consistent hypotheses. This is not always the case however; some theoretical scientists work in industry and perform valuable tasks resulting in important scientific advances that benefit mankind. The ones this book deals with do not!

1

INTRODUCTION

Higher education is a good thing; obtaining an advanced degree in a scientific field is a desirable aspiration for many. Today; however, the scientific method is quite often being abused. There is a lot of nonsense that is being fed to the public by pseudo-scientists, that includes pseudo-engineers, pseudo-physicists and pseudo-mathematicians among others; mostly those with PhD's, who think that they know more than everyone else due to their advanced degrees. This is not true of all scientists and mathematicians, but unfortunately, it is true for many of the most prominent and respected ones with the greatest influence on politicians, media and the general public.

Having a PhD does not necessarily imply that an individual is smarter than everyone else. In fact, the vast majority of those with PhDs are no smarter than the average person and a few are even of below average intelligence. A PhD is not synonymous with genius! A PhD only signifies that the holder of the advanced degree did the work necessary to obtain his advanced diploma. Having a PhD in a particular academic discipline does not qualify an individual as an expert in that entire field. Study is limited to a small area in a chosen field that requires a thesis of publishable quality on independent research. Most of the incorrect information being

1

disseminated today is due to false assumptions made by these scientists and engineers based on unproven and unchallenged scientific theories. Frequently science is distorted for political or economic gain, or errors are perpetuated by arrogance. More often than not, a recent college graduate will accept an unproven theory taken for granted during his studies and try to expand on it without questioning the validity of the original hypothesis, thereby perpetuating the myth.

Rene Descartes, the 17th century philosopher that is regarded as the father of modern philosophy, is famous for his statement on existence that declares "I think; therefore I am". There may be some truth in this proclamation, but it obviously does not encompass everything that exists. Many animals, all plants and inanimate objects such as rocks exist as well, but do not think; thinking is not a prerequisite for existing. Conversely, the slogan of many pseudo-scientists should be "I believe; therefore it is true", since they often assert that their unsupported theories are factual without veracity. Many believe that the majority rules and that this somehow justifies their assumption without verification or a preponderance of evidence to support their claim. Just because someone has an advanced degree in a particular scientific area does not qualify them as an expert in all scientific endeavors.

A scientific theory is supposed to be based on something that was observed by the one proposing the theory and that appears to be a valid explanation of a phenomenon that is supported by observation, reasoning and experimentation, not a wild guess without credible backup. Everyone is entitled to have their own opinions, but not their own facts. In our empirical world there is no alternate reality. A fact, which is the basis of the scientific method, does not change. A theory, however; implies something that is unproven or speculative that has not been confirmed. Quite often, many scientists will affirm that a particular supposition is

2

fact when in actuality most of them do not possess expertise in that particular field and are making their assertion based on a biased opinion. More recently, some pseudo-scientists have come up with the preposterous idea of utilizing what they call a "structured expert judgment exercise". When their computerized mathematical models and theories fail or are suspect, a few "experts" get together and make a "rational decision" on a subject and then declare it to be true. A theory does not become fact just because most scientists believe it is true or have decided upon majority vote that it is true. Unfortunately, in many cases, that is exactly what is being done in our scientific community today.

2

SIGNIFICANT ERRORS IN THE THEORY OF DARWINIAN EVOLUTION

According to many pseudo-scientists, all life evolved from a primordial slime that began life in the oceans millions of years ago and progressed to all the life forms that we observe on Earth today. In reality, there are a significant number of reasons why that is not only improbable, but utterly impossible.

There is a widespread belief that all human life began in the sea, crawled up on the land and progressed in distinct stages to our present state. Supposedly, these first animals and plants consisted of bacteria and later blue-green algae (cyanobacteria). This view is often attributed to Darwin, but in actuality, Darwin proposed the theory that life began on land in volcanic mud pots and not in the sea. There is not a shred of evidence that any of this actually happened; it is an absurd belief and there is considerable proof that this is not true. It is certainly not scientific. Scientifically impossible events are not made possible solely by the passage of time as evolutionists would have you believe. It is quite evident today that natural selection has not eradicated all the unintelligent human beings that don't possess the least amount of common sense. There are still more than enough to go around.

The pseudo-scientists; in this case representing themselves as "Evolutionary Biologists", would have you believe Darwin's "Tree of Life" as depicted in his book "On the Origin of Species" as an ever-growing representation that all species on Earth have a distinct position on this tree, evolving from a common ancestor. So if the first living organisms were bacteria, where are the plants on this "Tree of Life", and how did they evolve from these micro-organisms? Supposedly, one of the first rudimentary animals that arose from the primordial slime somehow decided that it would be better suited for survival if it anchored itself in the mud and obtained its nourishment from the soil and the sun by means of photosynthesis. At this time there was no soil that contained the decomposed organic matter that provides nutrients for plants, only raw chemicals and maybe some amino acids. Furthermore, how did these first plants obtain the means to utilize photosynthesis? This is a complex process that could not be solved in the time frame necessary for the newly formed plant to survive. Environmentalists state that there wasn't enough oxygen in the air for land animals to breathe so the plants transformed the entire atmosphere before the mammals could evolve. The theory goes that all plant life can be traced back to one tiny alga that ingested cyanobacteria eons ago and used photosynthesis to turn carbon dioxide and water into glucose and give off oxygen as a waste product, hence transforming the entire atmosphere into one rich in oxygen. What total nonsense!

Unfortunately for evolutionists, there are life forms that exist on Earth today that cannot be convincingly placed on this imaginary "Tree of Life"; they just do not fit into their scheme. For instance penguins look a lot like birds, but obviously are not. For one thing, they are too heavy to fly. True birds have hollow bones and are lightweight, a distinct requirement for flight. Also, penguins don't have wings. The appendages on their bodies that resemble wings are actually flippers that provide great dexterity in water, not air.

Today, Darwin's theory of evolution has a great following by not only people with a scientific background, but by many lay people that have no understanding of Darwin's concept or choose not to ascribe to a belief in Creationism. The majority of these so called "evolutionists" have never read Darwin's book entitled "The Origin of Species by means of Natural Selection or, the Preservation of Favored Races in the Struggle for Life" published by Charles Darwin November 22, 1859. If they had read his thesis on evolution, they would see that he uses the majority of the book in a vain attempt to convince the reader of his predetermined conclusion that all life is related and has descended from a common ancestor that miraculously arose from "warm little ponds" with no apparent rationale or assistance.

Although Darwin's book is 490 pages in length, the majority of the content of his book details his observations during his short time as a naturalist in the mid 19th century and not on corroborating his theory per se. He is constantly referring to contradictory examples of occurrences in nature that he manipulates to arrive at his predetermined conclusions. While claiming that Creationism manifests itself as "the blindness of preconceived opinion", he states "I should without hesitation adapt this view, even if it were unsupported by other facts or arguments" while professing that "our ignorance of the laws of variation is profound" and "I am inclined to believe in this truth although it rests on no direct evidence". He cannot with any degree of certainty distinguish between species, sub-species, breeds, sub-breeds, varieties, races, genera, sub-genera or inherited characteristics of plants or animals. When he cannot come up with adequate convincing evidence of his hypothesis through his observations, he often states "but I have not space here to enter on details on this subject". How convenient! He consistently states in nearly every chapter "it seems to me", "possibly" and "I strongly suspect". His assumption is that changes in species are effected unconsciously and gradually without the unknown element of a distinct act of creation and without the belief that a supreme being created primal forms capable of self development. He gives the weak argument that there "probably has been more extinction during periods of subsidence and more variation during periods of elevation" and that the geological record is extremely imperfect as his reasons for why we don't find intermediate varieties between fully evolved species. Even simple single cell organisms are extremely complex and are composed of numerous biological machines that Darwin was unaware of during his lifetime. In postulating his theory of evolution without an awareness of the complex nature of microbiology or an understanding of DNA, he could not have envisioned the immense complexity of even the simplest of life forms.

A later work by Steve Jones, a professor of genetics at the University College of London titled "Darwin's Ghost" was published in the year 2000. This book is an attempt to provide an updated analysis of Charles Darwin's work to account for all the scientific advances made since then. The premise was to provide evidence that Darwin's assumptions are as valid today as they were when he originally published his works. The book consists of 350 pages of small type and is difficult to read. This is mainly due to his extensive use of "purple prose" with extravagant and ornate use of adjectives and reference to places and things for which most readers would need a dictionary. Examples of such words are "ichneumonidae", "Osteodontokeratic Culture", "axolotl", "tucutucu", "edentate" and "eft" as well as countless others are referred to throughout his text. Additionally, he is addicted to the use of extremely long sentences, many more than 100 words in length, frequently resulting in loss of clarity. Attention is consequently drawn away from the narrative. A number of his quotations do not lend credence to the positions he is trying to convey. Examples are "Genes, like names, can be used to make guesses about the past", "Darwinism has a lot of explaining to do concerning repetitive DNA", "In less than a century the surface of the Earth had been so blurred that the record of the past is almost lost". Additionally, he refers to dates in the past when certain events have supposedly occurred as if they are indeed facts; in many cases referring to events that transpired "300 million years ago" or "half a billion years ago". His entire work contains reference to remarks describing evolution employing such language as "perhaps", "nobody knows", "speculation", "so evolutionists guess", "makes no sense", "waiting to be discovered", "was thought to have", "might be", and "if they are right", yet he describes Creationism as "blindness of preconceived opinion" as stated by Darwin himself. It would appear that he is also blinded by a preconceived notion of the atheists' religion of Evolution without providing any new evidence of its validity.

Both Darwin and Jones refer to events that supposedly occurred thousands, million or even billions of years ago as if they were there or had some kind of direct knowledge of these prehistoric happenings. While Darwin believes that evolution is a slow gradual process and that less developed species change slowly and more advanced life forms mutate at a more rapid pace, Jones believes that extremely rapid evolution also occurs in lower life forms such as viruses. He gives the rapid changes in the AIDS virus to accommodate changing conditions as an example of a more recent phenomenon; something that Darwin did not experience in his day. Both Darwin and Jones basic belief is that natural selection acts to preserve and accumulate minor advantages through genetic mutation brought about by the organic life form's primary goal of survival. While Darwin and Jones may be able to exhibit a compelling argument that individual species may change over time to better adapt to changing conditions in climate or other environmental issues, they none-the-less never reveal any indication of one species changing into another.

In light of the recent tremendous advances made in genetics, biochemistry and molecular biology Darwin's theory of evolution is not only suspect but virtually impossible. Today it is known that the tiniest bacterial cells although incredibly small contain thousands of pieces of intricate molecular machinery made up of billions of atoms without parallel in the inorganic world that are extremely complicated. At the time that Darwin developed his theory of evolution, no one was aware of the complex nature of microbiology or the existence of DNA. It is known today that all items in the Universe are composed of atoms consisting of electrons, neutrons and protons as well as even smaller sub-atomic particles. Although the arrangement of atomic particles is different for each chemical element, it is now believed that these atomic and sub-atomic particles are identical and are the building blocks for the countless atoms that constitute all mater in the Cosmos, organic and inorganic. Likewise, although DNA comprises the building blocks of life and there is little difference between the DNA of monkeys, apes or humans, it does not mean that we are all related through evolution. In the grand scheme of things, it is probable that similar to the atomic and sub-atomic universe, DNA contains the generic code for all life without regard for any relationship between different species. Moreover, life has a blueprint with intelligent design that is formed from a double helix structure known as DNA (deoxyribonucleic acid). DNA is found in the nucleus of the cell and contains the biological instruction that makes each species unique. Scientists have only been able to decipher about 5% of the total DNA strand, so they have declared the remaining 95% useless. How incredibly egotistical is that, to believe that because they have not been smart enough to determine the reason for the majority of the DNA strand, that it does not have a purpose and is junk! More recently, it has been shown that although this so called junk DNA may not contain code for new proteins as in a regular gene, some provide essential regulatory features in the cell, such as keeping a heart beating. That is certainly an important function! In time, it is likely that the remaining 95% of the DNA code that is presently a mystery will be decoded and found to contain valuable information, not erroneous junk. Life does not materialize from random selection as the theory of Darwinian Evolution would have you believe. Intelligent design is involved. Spontaneous generation of life has been utterly disproved although pseudo-scientists would have you believe otherwise.

One argument that evolutionists give for the validity of their theory that all animals are linked through evolution is the fact that the DNA of many animals are very similar and that even some animal parts can be transplanted into a human and survive, often providing valuable attributes. One good example of this is the fact that desiccated porcine (pig) thyroid can be ingested by humans to cure hypothyroidism when the human thyroid gland in under-active. This has been done for over 100 years with good success. It is true that the DNA of all mammals is very similar, but this argument needs to be taken one step further. The building blocks of animals and humans are noticeably similar. Changes in just a small number of regulatory genes can result in significant changes in an individual species, but cannot result in change into another species. Although all atoms of a kind are alike no matter what animal or plant they are found in, it is also factual that the sub-atomic particles that these atoms are comprised of, i.e. electrons, protons, neutrons, quarks and all other sub-atomic particles are identical for all atoms whether or not they are animal, vegetable or mineral. Using the same logic as evolutionists, not only are humans related to animals and plants, but also rocks and everything else in the entire Cosmos. This is implausible!

No one has ever been able to create the simplest life form on Earth even though the best conditions for doing so are found here. There is evidence that some simple life forms, in particular bacteria, mutate into different strains of bacteria. This; however, is not evolution, only adaptation to changes in their environment. They are still bacteria. There are no known instances of one species ever evolving into a completely different species as they would have us believe. Even the simplest single cell organism is immensely complex and contains DNA in its cell nucleus that can only be there through intelligent design, not random evolutionary processes.

Many life forms occasionally adapt to modest changes in their environment, but more often than not if the change is too great, the species is not able to cope with the change in the environment and goes extinct. There is considerable proof of this happening all around us throughout history. Well over 90% of all species of plants and animals that have ever lived on Earth are now extinct. Human beings are the only exception to this rule since man is the only animal with the ability to modify his surroundings when threatened with fundamental changes in his environment. Man is the only animal with the mental prowess to transform his environment to meet his requirements or desires. No other animal has ever been able to build the complex structures or machines or communicate through written or spoken language as mankind. Man, although an animal in structure, is vastly superior to any other plant or animal in the organic community. Man is the only animal that is able to reason or contemplate his own existence. Human beings are unique within the animal kingdom.

Many scientists today believe that humans were created through evolutionary progression from earlier life forms. The obviously flaw in this assumption comes from the fact that not only are there no credible records of intermediate species between any lower life forms and humans, but the immense different between all varieties of animals and plants collectively in comparison to humans. The main concern with all plants and animals is finding food and procreation to perpetuate the species. There is a greater similarity between all plants and animals excluding man than the comparison of man with any other species.

Humans, or the species Homo sapiens, is unique in comparison to all other life forms. Humans exhibit cognitive abilities with memory as well as language capacity, reasoning and planning abilities not present in all other life forms. The intelligence of humans that includes self-awareness, learning ability, emotions, planning, creativity and problem solving far exceeds that of any other species.

No plant or animal has ever altered their environment in a significant way to improve their living conditions as man has. Some animals exhibit a rudimentary ability to use crude natural implements such as rocks or sticks, but not anywhere close to what the human species has achieved or is capable of. OK, so there is an elephant that can paint with his trunk and is capable of artwork that in some subjective opinions matches or exceeds several of Pablo Picasso's later cubism period works and costs peanuts in comparison. This animal has; however, been trained by humans and probably has no comprehension of what he is actually doing. Additionally the elephant is not capable of creating the implements, such as the paints, brushes and canvas required to perform this feat and would not do so on his own outside of captivity.

No living being or organism other than humans has remotely achieved any of man's accomplishments or has altered his environment so significantly. Only the human race has ever created language, writing and music, domesticated fire, created the wheel, mastered mathematics, science and medicine, created the telephone, radio, television and the internet, invented automobiles, airplanes and traveled to the Moon to mention only a few of humans prowess over his environment. The immense gap between all living organisms and man's accomplishments is astounding. Evolution cannot begin to explain this contradiction with its underlying perspective of an unbroken chronological succession of species.

For evolution from one species to another to take place, first a simple living life form would have to be created purely through natural chemical processes in a nutrient rich environment without any help from another living organism. There are numerous reasons why this is not possible. The first singular cell life form would have to be not only self sustaining, but capable of self reproduction with only chemical nourishment. A virus or parasite needs a host to exist and therefore does not qualify as the first potential living organism. Remember, that at this time no other life form exists on the planet, not only animals, but plants as well. So what is this new first life form going to consume as food if no other plant or animal exists? How long can it survive and reproduce without a food source? Cells are composed of complex arrangements of chemicals including amino acids, lipids and sugars among others. This is a simplification; significantly more is required. The cell must be able to store information and pass it on to its self replicated cell through DNA code. The DNA would have to contain the correct programming to pass on the characteristics of the original life form. Where does this coded DNA come from if not from an intelligent source? The minimal number of codes required for the simplest life form to exist and reproduce is staggering. All of this must be accomplished within a total chemical environment without any outside help. The probability against life being formed by chance this way without any intelligent intervention is overwhelming.

Even something as incredibly simple as a chicken egg is in reality so complex as to not have the slightest possibility of being created through chance alone. An egg shell is composed nearly completely of calcium carbonate with more than fifteen thousand minute pores that allow air and moisture to enter while thin inner and outer protein membranes exclude bacteria and dust. The egg white, known as the albumen, consists of layers composed of about forty different proteins and water. The yolk is held in the center of the egg by two rope like structures that connect the yolk's external membrane to the inner lining of the shell. The yellow egg yolk contains more protein than the white and most of the vitamins and minerals, fatty acids and antioxidants, and if fertilized will produce a chick. To become fertilized, the hen that lays the egg must mate and store the deposited rooster sperm in a small internal pouch. When the newly formed egg passes by, it is fertilized by this sperm, develops the shell and is laid. At this time, the fertilized egg will have already developed on the order of 20,000 embryonic cells. Furthermore, to develop into a fully formed chick, this egg must contain all the DNA coding required, but part comes from the hen and part from the rooster. Without both parts of this genetic code, the egg will not be fertilized. Where did the first chicken hen and rooster come from? This is only one simple example; there are many considerably more complex living things including man. Did all of this happen through random mutations? It is extremely unlikely!

The eye is another example of an extremely complex structure that could not have been created by chance. Even Charles Darwin stated in 1872 that "To suppose that the eye could have been formed by natural selection seems, I freely confess, absurd in the highest possible degree".

More often than not in recent times when viewing any supposedly scientific natural history program on TV, the host declares that a particular animal has evolved from a different species to arrive in its current form. They do this on a regular basis although they have absolutely no evidence to back up this ridiculous assumption. For instance they say that a particular humming bird species has evolved its longer bill to obtain the nectar from a long tubular flower from one with a shorter bill that existed earlier and obtained nectar from a shorter tubed flower. Who is to say that the deeper tubed flower only came into being more recently than the shorter tubed flower, or that the long billed bird didn't exist during the same time as the shorter billed one, or even before it? There is a synergistic relationship between the long billed humming bird and the deep flower; they require each other for survival. One could not exist prior to the existence of the other. Where did this information come from; obviously from someone's imagination, certainly not from verifiable fact?

Another absurd assumption that is often made is that a particular species of animal crossed a land bridge from one continent to another millions of years ago. They argue that this is why some animals exist on nearby continents or islands and not others. Even if this was true, it doesn't explain which continent the animal originated on and which one it traveled to. For instance they try to convince us that the leopard migrated from India to Sri Lanka and that is why it is found there. This may be true, but who is to say that, if it did make this journey, it didn't originate in Sri Lanka and migrate to India Where is the proof? There is none; it is all unsubstantiated speculation. It is certainly not scientific fact.

If a change in the environment is not major enough to threaten extinction, what is the incentive for a simple life form to make a crucial change in its ability to live in a foreign environment? These simple life forms do not possess complex enough brains, if any, to make this kind of decision in the first place, deliberately or unconsciously. Also, according to the theory of evolution, the change would take hundreds to millions of years to occur. That would require hundreds to thousands of generations of the particular life form to evolve into the new variety. That is highly unlikely and there is no fossil record of there being any intermediate life forms. Paleontologists often equate finding a single piece of bone that they are unable to identify with the discovery of an entirely new species. This does not constitute a remarkable scientific discovery as they would like you to believe as it takes a highly imaginative individual to create an entirely new species from a single bone fragment. This is all speculation without the scientific method being applied and not a shred of evidence to back up their ridiculous claim. All fossils are found completely formed either in an earlier extinct configuration or a more recent variety. No intermediate "missing link" has ever been discovered.

No scientific facts or fossil evidence exists that prove the veracity of any prehistoric man propagated by evolutionists, anthropologists, archaeologists, paleontologists or the media. All are fictitious and a product of man's imagination. The Piltdown man, Nebraska man, Java man, Pekin man, Neanderthal man, The Taung child, Ranapithecus, Australopithecines, Lucy, and Ardi have all been proven to be hoaxes perpetuated by evolutionists in a frenzied attempt at proving their flawed theory. The Piltdown man's skull turned out to be human with an orangutan's jaw and a chimp's teeth. The reconstruction of the Nebraska man, including a representation of his entire family, was based on a single tooth which was ultimately discovered to be that of an extinct species of wild pig. The Neanderthal man was later determined to be totally human and it was established that the alleged age of this so-called pre-human skull was a lie. In actuality, the skull was revealed to be about 1,300 years old, not over 21,000 years old as originally purported. Lucy is one of the latest of the so called discoveries and was the subject of some of the most rigorous conjecture as the oldest and most complete fossil of an early humanoid ever found. After further investigation, it appears that one of the bones in this "ancient skeleton" actually belonged to a baboon. Lucy's hands and feet are depicted by "Evolutionists" as human like, but no hand or foot bones were ever found. Hardly anyone ever speaks out about these obvious deceptions because of peer pressure and personal attacks on anyone that challenges the main foundation of the pseudo-archaeologists faulty assumptions. No "missing link" between any two species has ever been found to exist. If evolution is a continuous process that occurs over a considerable period of time, there should be a substantial preponderance of evidence to corroborate their existence. There is none!

More recently "scientists" say they have discovered a humanoid creature that was about three feet tall in a cave in the Philippines that supposedly lived 50 to 67 thousand years ago. They make this claim based on a few small hand and foot bones, a partial leg bone and teeth that they discovered. First, their estimate of this humanoid living 50 to 67 thousand years ago is extremely suspect. This discrepancy of 17,000 years represents a 25% error (equivalent to over 200 human life spans). Not only is it only impossible to accurately determine ages this far in the past with any degree of certainty, but it is impossible to construct an accurate rendition of any creature with this small of a sample.

Again, it is likely that this will be proven to either be a complete hoax or will be attributed to a more recent known animal species.

It is a known fact that many of the species of plants on Earth require bees, other insects, or animals to reproduce by pollination. Recently it has been observed that a decrease in the honey bee population significantly reduced certain crops that are dependent upon them for cross pollination since the bees transfer the pollen from one plant to another on their bodies. How could these plants evolve or even survive long enough to reproduce unless the bees were developed at the same time as the plants? There is a synergy where the plants are dependent upon the insects for their survival and vice versa. It is not reasonable to believe that both the insects and the plants evolved at the same moment in time to make this synergistic relationship possible. In nature everything is interconnected with many interrelated pieces that collectively make up the whole. Prior to this synergy, how did they survive at all if this evolutionary process takes millions, thousands or even only a few years? It is not only unsubstantiated, but unfeasible.

According to the Second Law of Thermodynamics, entropy always increases in a closed system. This means that all course of action manifests a tendency toward disintegration and decay; something that is easily observed in the real world. For evolution from a lesser state of being to a greater one, entropy would have to decrease. It is true; however, that not everything in the Universe must always increase in entropy. Small temporary decreases in entropy within closed systems such as refrigeration systems have been observed on Earth, but for entropy to decrease, an equal increase in entropy must occur within another part of the system. There is a preponderance of evidence to verify that overall entropy increases and that the total entropy of the Universe can never decrease. We have all witnessed the disintegration and breakdown of matter in everyday situations in our daily lives. How do these so called scientists explain the decrease in entropy that was necessary to form all the stars and planets, and to bring about evolution? That's easy! According to the pseudo-scientists, we are to believe that previously, entropy decreased until all their predictions came true, then it reversed. Is that a reasonable assumption?

According to the "Knowledge Doubling Curve" created by Buckminster Fuller, up until around the twentieth century it was believed that the world's knowledge base doubled every century. By the end of World War II, during the late 1940's, it purportedly doubled in about 25 years. By the early twenty-first century, the world's information base doubled every two years, or less. By the year 2020, it is expected to double every 72 hours. Recently, it was declared that currently, every two days as much data is generated as was created from the beginning of time until 2003. These are, of course, estimates and may vary considerably, but much of the assimilation of information is the result of the internet and the resulting worldwide availability of information. This time frame is much too short to have been caused by evolution; the human brain's capacity could not have increased due to the effects of evolution so rapidly. Additionally, this doubling of information is not the same as the doubling of knowledge, as they would have you believe. Knowledge implies that something useful can be done with it; not necessarily information or raw data per se. The assimilation of knowledge takes considerably longer.

In reality, the human brain capacity has always been about the same, only the comprehension of the world around us was much less in the past. Today, there is a much better understanding of scientific issues than there was even one hundred years ago by some, but the majority of people even today are not all that knowledgeable in the fields of science or technology. There were many highly educated individuals in the past that in spite of their limited background were able to lay the basic groundwork for all the increases in science that we see today. Many of these people were much smarter than the majority of the people living today. They had to do all this research without the aid of computers and advanced scientific principles. Their scientific discoveries made it possible for most of our modern conveniences to be envisioned, and these highly motivated individuals such as Thomas Edison, Alexander Graham Bell, Nikola Tesla, George Westinghouse and others, invented many of these beneficial commodities as well.

There were great minds in the past that gave us things such as classical music, traditional art and scientific knowledge that are not being duplicated today. How many musical pieces, works of art and scientific discoveries, such as those produced by Beethoven, Mozart, Strauss, Leonardo de Vinci, Michelangelo, Newton or Galileo to mention just a few do we see today? Regardless of individual tastes, are we really to believe that now days those producing modern art, some of which is unrecognizable that a child could duplicate, or rock music and rap with only minimal lyrics and a limited vocabulary are in the same league with what the masters produced centuries ago without the technology we have today? Our human brain has not increased in volume or ability through this so called miracle of evolution; we have just increased our assimilation of knowledge through the greater availability of information. There is plenty of room to increase our knowledge base by adaptation without resorting to evolution. One of the largest brains on record belonged to a moron, not a genius!

Today many of our high school graduates can operate a computer or cell phone with ease, but cannot do simple math, even addition or subtraction, much less multiplication or division. Many students demonstrate poor academic performance due to unqualified chronically ineffective teachers. Today, academic standards in schools have been reduced considerably in order to make it easier for one to graduate due to poor student performance and lack of ambition. In the United States, a short a time as 40 years ago, a C average student would be capable of an A average today. Also, in sports, there are instances of students receiving trophies just for attendance without ever having to achieve excellence as was previously the requirement. Today, many are deemed heroes based only on their profession without ever having performed an act of bravery.

In a survey of over 2,000 people conducted as recently as 2012, twenty six percent of Americans were not aware that the Earth orbits the Sun. There are people that still believe that the Earth is flat that have their own organization known as "The Flat Earth Society". A recent poll showed that about one fifth of all Americans could not locate the United States on a world map, much less other countries, continents or oceans, demonstrating their geographic illiteracy. All evidence shows that on the whole human intelligence is decreasing due to shorter attention spans, poor learning habits and an increase in individuals with mental problems, when according to evolutionists humans should be getting smarter. This is not evidence of evolution at work!

It's no wonder that it is so easy to dupe the public into believing these untruths since, even today, the majority of the population has no interest in travel outside the borders of their own country, much less, curiosity in the Solar System or the Universe. Considerably more than half of the population of the United States does not have a passport and have never traveled outside the borders of their country of birth. Although the oceans of the Earth make up over 70 percent of the surface area, even today we know more about the Moon than we do about the seas of our own planet.

To summarize, what are some of the major facts that challenge the theory of evolution and support intelligent design?

1. There are numerous species of plant and animal life that do not fit on Darwin's imaginary "Tree of Life".

2. There is not a shred of evidence that life began in the sea or mud pots from which all life evolved.

3. Spontaneous generation of life has been disproved. Life has never been created by man in the laboratory even under the absolute best of conditions.

4. Well over 90% of all plant and animal species that ever lived on Earth are now extinct. They could not undergo the transformations necessary to evolve.

5. There is a synergistic relationship between many plants and animals that could not occur unless both partners in this relationship evolved at the same time.

6. There is no legitimate fossil evidence that confirms prehistoric man ever existed.

7. There are no intermediate life forms. All fossils are found completely formed either in an earlier extinct configuration or a more recent variety.

8. The structure of DNA is so complex that it could not have been created by random natural selection regardless of the extent of the time-span as proposed by the theory of evolution.

3

LIMITATIONS ON SPACE TRAVEL & THE LAWS OF PHYSICS, CHEMISTRY & MATHEMATICS

During the entire lifetime of the human race we have never ventured further that the surface of our own moon, and that was done only twelve times over a four year span. The last time anyone visited the Moon was over 42 years ago! The Moon is only approximately 240,000 miles away from the Earth. We envision visiting the planet Mars, but presently do not have the necessary technology since this planet's average distance from Earth is about 140 million miles, or over 580 times the distance between our Earth and the Moon. Since the Earth and Mars orbit the Sun at different speeds and both planets travel in elliptical orbits, the closest distance that the two planets come to each other is about 35 million miles. That is still about 146 times the distance between Earth and our nearest neighbor, the Moon. The most powerful propulsion systems our scientific minds have devised to date consist of liquid and solid fueled rocket engines that are extremely large, dangerous and expensive with only a very limited range. These engines utilize chemical reactions to produce thrust and are incredibly inefficient. The top speed of an unmanned craft to date is only about 37,000 mph with the speed of a manned one even slower. That is over 18,000 times slower than the speed of light! A light year is the distance that light travels in a perfect vacuum in one year at approximately 186,282 miles per second. This translates to about 5.88 trillion miles/light year (186,282 miles/sec. x 60 sec./min. x 60 min./hr. x 24 hr./day x 365.25 days/year). Recently a manmade unmanned object has finally traveled from Earth to the edge of our Solar System. With our present technology, this monumental feat took 36 years! Obviously, we have a long way to go to even come close to the speed required for deep space travel.

To the best of our knowledge, our entire Solar System exists as only a small formation located between two of the spiral arms of our Milky Way Galaxy and is situated approximately 60 percent of the way from the center of our galaxy. Our astronomer's best guess is that the Milky Way Galaxy is about 100 light years in diameter and contains about 300 billion stars, with numerous planets and moons. They are constantly revising this approximation upwards with new evidence since these estimates are only guesses. No one has ever been able to accurately count the number of stars in the night sky since they are not all visible and are so incredibly far from Earth. It is estimated that on average roughly 5,000 stars are visible on a clear, dark, moonless night when viewed with the naked eye. The most being a little more than 9,000 since it has been established that the dimmest light that is visible to the typical human eye is an apparent magnitude of 6.5. For anyone from Earth to travel to Proxima Centauri, the closest and dimmest star in Alpha Centauri, our nearest trinary star system that is only slightly over four light years away, at a speed of even 50,000 miles per hour that far exceeds our present technological capability for manned flight, would take over 57,000 years. The new generation of heavy lift chemical rockets presently in the development stage will not appreciably increase that speed. Even if fusion becomes a viable power source some day, a speed of only about ten percent of the speed of light is likely obtainable and it would still take 43 years to reach Alpha Centauri. We would need to not only be able to reach a habitable environment in a reasonable time, but also be able to sustain life, including air, water and food as well as a suitable environment for long term travel in space. Our life spans are far too short to ever consider space travel outside our Solar System unless we develop significantly more highly advanced technology and considerably more efficient and powerful propulsion systems. Our present state of the art propulsion systems consist of chemical rockets that are an extraordinarily inefficient use of energy. Even then, due to the vastness of space and the extreme distances involved, we are severely limited in how far we can travel at any speed that we could achieve. It is highly unlikely that we will ever be able to travel at or considerably faster than the speed of light. Even if it were possible, due to the vast galactic distances involved just to reach Andromeda, our nearest galaxy, at 100 times light speed would take 25,000 years.

Some scientists, mostly mathematicians and so called theoretical scientists talk about folding space and wormholes as if they are fact, but in reality, are only figments of their imagination. When they talk about folding space and transversing a shorter distance through a wormhole, they describe the Universe as a flat plane that can be bent over on itself when in fact; at least within the confines of the Universe that is visible from Earth, it is three dimensional. They would like us to believe that space is like the surface of a balloon that is continually expanding. That would make outer space two dimensional with a limited flat surface third dimension to allow it to be folded; however, wherever one looks, the Universe is homogeneous and isotropic with an even distribution of matter and energy. No one has ever been able to adequately describe how empty space could be folded over on itself. Also, no one has ever seen a wormhole; it is purely imaginary and has only been created by so called theoretical-mathematicians. Even they believe it would take unimaginable amounts of energy to create one and that it would be unstable and short lived. Besides, if they could create one, they haven't solved the problem as to where we would wind up on the other end or how we would ever be able to return. If you don't know where you are going to end up and cannot return, how do you know there is a place that is suitable to sustain human life at your destination? You better solve this problem before you leave!

If you can't shorten the distance, then you must travel at a very high rate of speed to get to where you are trying to go in a reasonable length of time. According to the most recently accepted scientific theories, nothing can exceed the speed of light (in a vacuum) and, as you approach the speed of light, mass increases and it takes increasingly more energy, until you reach a limit due to the amount of energy required becoming unachievable. Even, if you could overcome this problem, you would have to overcome the problem of the excessive acceleration required to reach this speed in a reasonable interval of time. Other than the light speed limitation, there doesn't seem to be any other practical limit as to the speed humans can travel; the planet Earth is travelling in orbit around the Sun at a constant speed of about 66,600 miles per hour, but we are not aware of it because of the lack of the inertial force of acceleration. The problem is getting up to the speed required to make any deep space travel even to the nearest star system possible. Humans are very fragile beings and cannot be accelerated too rapidly or they will be crushed to death by excessive inertial forces. Long before this point is reached it will become too uncomfortable for humans to endure this extreme acceleration for the long periods of time required to attain the necessary velocity to make deep space exploration practical. When considering travel at a high velocity, two factors, those of acceleration and jerk must be taken to account. Acceleration is the steady state increase of velocity with respect to time; also known as the second derivative (d^2s/dt^2) of displacement (s) and the first derivative (dv/dt) of velocity (v). Jerk is the rate of change of acceleration with respect to time; also known as the third derivative (d^3s/dt^3) of displacement, the second derivative of velocity (d^2v/dt^2) and the first derivative of acceleration (da/dt). Humans are capable of traveling at virtually any velocity within limits (steady state speed in a straight line) as no additional forces are imposed upon the body. This is one of the basic principles of relativity whereby the person in the spacecraft experiences forces relative to the vessel, not outside their frame of reference. The problem arises when acceleration, jerk and/or changes in direction are introduced; these are forces that are not adequately tolerated by the human body if they are excessive. To travel at an extremely high velocity, that velocity must first be reached which requires acceleration to obtain the desired steady state speed. Although a human can withstand considerable inertial forces for short periods of time, a comfortable rate of linear or lateral acceleration for a human to endure for an extended period of time is about 0.15G where (G) is the gravitational force on Earth of approximately 32 ft/sec², and 0.15G is just under 5 ft/sec². At this rate of acceleration, just to reach $1/10^{th}$ light speed in the vacuum of space would take 228 days, or more than $6/10^{th}$ of a year of constant acceleration; and that is only $1/10^{th}$ the speed of light (just over 67 million miles/hr). Even this low continuous rate of acceleration could probably not be tolerated for this long a time. At this speed, it would still take approximately 43 years to reach Proxima Centauri, the closest star to our solar system. In this example, jerk would only come into play during the time required to reach the constant rate of acceleration of 5 ft/sec^2. Also, in space a constant velocity can be maintained almost indefinitely, but acceleration requires that a force be applied continuously to the spacecraft until the desired velocity is reached (F=MA). Presently, there is no propulsion system that can provide this necessary acceleration for anywhere near the time required to reach the high velocities necessary for deep space exploration.

An added problem is that space is not totally empty; there are stray hydrogen gas atoms and micrometeoroids. Although the density of these hydrogen atoms range from about one per cubic centimeter to one per cubic meter depending on one's location, at high speeds they become lethal and bombard a spacecraft and crew with intense radiation. Micrometeoroids, if encountered could severely damage the vessel beyond repair or kill the occupants. Another concern is with radiation from the Sun or any other nearby star that is approached. Humans are protected from the extreme radiation from our Sun by the Earth's magnetic field. Once that field is left, the radiation being absorbed by persons in space is excessive and over time will prove fatal. Having somehow overcome these problems, and assuming that you can reach nine-tenths of the speed of light (over 600 million miles per hour) in a reasonable amount of time without excessive discomfort, how far can you go in say 20 years? In the context of the human life span, this is a long time for anyone to be traveling through space in order to reach a destination that they will not be able to return to Earth from. This is only 18 light years, or a small fraction of the way to the center of our own Milky Way Galaxy, not to mention the hundreds to billions of light years required to reach other galaxies in the total expanse of our Universe, if indeed the distances are as great as many of our scientists believe they are. Also, don't forget that, if these scientists are correct, the

Universe is expanding away from us, making this feat even more difficult, if not totally impossible. In reality, these space travelers could return to Earth, but what would be the point? It would take at least another 20 years, so they would probably be at least 60 years old and nothing would be recognizable when they returned because according to Einstein's general theory of relativity, time moves more quickly in a gravitational field than it does in one lacking gravitation, so while the space travelers would have aged only about 40 years, due to time dilation and length contraction, the Earth and its inhabitants would have aged considerably more during the astronaut's space exploration.

Another concern with space travel is navigation, or more accurately, the lack of it. When traveling within the confines of our Solar System, we have earthbound navigational aids to guide us. A spacecraft in our Solar System uses precisely coordinated radio signals to communicate with signals sent from Earth. Outside of the boundaries of our Solar System there presently is no deep space positioning system. Even though radio waves travel at the speed of light, distances are so great that radio transmissions in deep space take too long. Due to the immense distances involved, stars appear to remain stationary in space meaning that you can use them to inform you where to go, but not to tell where you are. We can determine our orientation in relation to Earth based on observations of the relative positions of the stars corresponding to the rotation of the Earth. This is not possible in interstellar or intergalactic space since navigation requires a frame of reference and we have multiple movable frames of reference in deep space depending on where we are located. This makes navigation from one reference frame, for instance Earth, to another ten to hundreds of light years away virtually impossible. What's more, since the rate of time change varies considerably with one's proximity to either a strong or weak gravitational force field, it is unlikely that you can determine what time it is at your location relative to someone in an extraneous gravitational region. There are no 24 hour days in deep space that correspond to our familiar time frame here on Earth; no separate days and nights and no applicable calendar. If one reaches another planet in a far away star system, there may be days, years and an appropriate local calendar, but they are in all probability indiscernible with those on Earth. There are TV serials and movies such as Star Trek, Star Wars, Battlestar Galactica, Farscape and others that portray a time frame that is appropriate in all locations visited within our galaxy with a suitable means of navigation in deep space, but this is only fabricated fiction without veracity.

One ridiculous concept for space travel is to create a large sail the size of Texas in space and use the solar wind to propel us to distance places. That is really big! If you have you ever driven across Texas, you would realize just how big. It would be so big and fragile that it would certainly have to be constructed in space. Even so, it would require a tremendous quantity of resources shuttled to the construction site at enormous cost. Even a sail the size of a major city, much less Texas, would be impractical. One problem, even if the sail could be constructed, is that space debris encountered over long distances could rip the sail apart leaving the space explorers stranded. It would be so delicate that acceleration and deceleration forces would have to be kept to a minimum to prevent its destruction from excessive inertial forces. Another problem with this notion is that when the space craft leaves the region of our Sun, where does the "solar wind" come from to continue the journey prior to reaching the vicinity of another star that could provide the necessary thrust? Yes, the spacecraft could continue to travel indefinitely at constant velocity, with negligible gravitational interaction, but where would the energy come from to provide acceleration if required?

If for some reason deceleration became necessary during the trip, how would the spacecraft resume a reasonable velocity to complete its mission? Photon flux density decreases as the inverse square of the distance from its source. So as the spacecraft gets further away from the solar source, considerably less force is generated until finally, there is insufficient thrust available to be practical. In reality, distances between all stars, planets and other stellar phenomenon are so extreme that when you leave our solar system, there is only open space and everything that can be observed is at extreme distances. Stars would look like dots of light and planets would not even be visible; you would find yourself all alone in a dark, empty space with no viable means of propulsion except for the momentum obtained earlier when the source was present.

Another concept is the use of anti-matter for a nearly inexhaustible fuel supply, but this proposal is strictly fantasy at this time. No one knows how to capture anti-matter, or even prove beyond reasonable doubt that it exists. Even if it does exist, no one can explain how it could be safely contained or used as a fuel for interstellar travel. How do you restrain something that will violently explode whenever it comes in contact with regular matter? The slightest breach in the containment system would result in total annihilation of the spacecraft.

Another proposal taken from the fictitious Hollywood production "Star Trek" is to use a "Warp Drive" to travel extreme distances in very short times. Warp drive is a hypothetical propulsion system that allows for faster than light speed. NASA Spaceflight recently made an announcement that it had successfully tested an EM (electromagnetic) drive that creates thrust without a corresponding opposite reaction. This, of course, violates Newton's third law of conservation of momentum. Again pseudo-scientists are just creating more bad science that they expect the public to believe.

Maybe someday man will be able to solve these problems and travel to distant star systems in a reasonable time frame, but not in the foreseeable future. Man has advanced considerably in his understanding of the Earth and our Solar System in just the past 100 years or so, but not in his understanding of the entire Universe. These pseudo-scientists would like us to believe that they can peer into space from this tiny corner of our galaxy and determine all there is to know about the entire Cosmos from the beginning of time. Not too long ago it was believed that the Earth was flat and at the center of the entire Universe. Before the Hubble telescope gave us views of outer space without the limitations imposed by the Earth's atmosphere, scientists thought the Milky Way Galaxy was the extent of our entire Universe. Now they believe there are billions of other galaxies that are millions to billions of light years from Earth. Are they correct this time? Maybe, but the Universe is just too vast and complex for man to understand fully without being able to actually go there and experience it firsthand. How do we know that the laws of physics, chemistry and mathematics that work in our corner of our galaxy are universal everywhere in the Cosmos if we have never been there? They probably are, but that is just another theory until proven beyond doubt to be fact.

Another factor that has been overlooked is that when you look at the night sky, if the distances are truly as great as many astronomers attest to, then everything that you see you are seeing as it was in the past, not the present. We do not see any stars or galaxies as they exist now. They are invisible to us and will never be observable from Earth in their present state. Even the light from our Sun takes about 8.3 minutes to reach Earth. Everything that is observed by eyesight happened in the past; we don't observe anything in the present. The light from an object one foot in front of one's eyes takes one nanosecond (one billionth of a second) to reach your eyes. Obviously, this time interval is too short to comprehend, as are all distances in common everyday experiences, but as the distance increases, so does the time required. This time becomes significant when cosmic distances are involved. Additionally, the light comings from the nearer stars are younger by far than the light from stars on the other side of the galaxy. What you see from Earth is not necessarily what is there now, and what you see from the farthest reaches of space is what was there considerably earlier than the closer objects that we can observe. Although improbable, most of what we see now may not have even existed during our entire lifetime, and the shape of the galaxies may not even be the same now as we are presently observing them from Earth. We can't even prove that the Milky Way Galaxy exists since when we look into the night sky what we think we see is a cross-section of the galaxy. It is most likely true, but since we will probably never be able to observe the Milky Way Galaxy from afar, we are only speculating on the shape of what is actually there based on the observed shapes of distant galaxies. Additionally, the astronomers haven't explained why the galaxies observed nearly at the alleged edge of the Cosmos appear fully formed. If the Big Bang places them nearer to the creation of the Universe, there should not be any fully established galaxies that far out. If the light we are seeing is from around 13 billion light-years ago as they profess, it should be seen as it once existed very early on in the Universe's beginning before any mature galaxies existed. We will never be able to see beyond the observable Universe if indeed the speed of light is constant. Based on a constant speed of light of 186,282 miles per second, the observable Universe, defined as the distance light can travel during our lifetime, is about 13.8 billion light-years. These scientists nevertheless claim that we can actually see considerably farther; approximately 46 billion light-years due to the apparent expansion of the Universe. They; however, do not offer any verifiable proof to confirm this theory. These hypothesis regarding time and distance made by theoretical physicists and mathematicians presuppose that light travels through space at a fixed velocity and requires a finite time to travel a fixed distance. It does not consider the hypotheses that the speed of light might be variable or travel from the source to the observer instantaneously. If it does, as some scientists maintain, this changes everything.

As human beings we are limited to what we can observe from our humble planet Earth that is part of our Solar System. Since we have never ventured very far from home, anything that we believe is true for the remainder of the Cosmos is just conjecture. It is assumed by most scientists that all our currently accepted laws of physics and mathematics apply to the entire Cosmos and that it has always been so, except for some exceptions made when their theories do not fit the facts. In these cases, instead of revising their theories, they chose to modify the laws of physics and mathematics temporarily to fit their theories. This is not how the scientific method works!

All science including physics, chemistry and mathematics among others are relatively new concepts that have come into existence only recently. The word science comes from Latin and means knowledge. Science was only created by natural philosophers in the early 1200s and the word scientist was coined only in the year 1812; just over 200 years ago. These terms have been created by man to try to understand our physical surroundings. Calculus and modern physics was not even invented until the seventeenth century, and the periodic table of chemical elements was not in existence prior to the late nineteenth century. In the beginning, many errors were made in an attempt to come up with working solutions that would better explain our environment.

Some of the greater minds, such as Isaac Newton, came up with numerous theories that fit very well with observations of our physical natural world. These theories still work quite well in solving most of our everyday physical tasks, as long as they are confined to our Earth with its atmosphere and gravitational forces, and if speeds are kept within reasonable limits. When variables such as those found beyond the confines of Earth in our Solar System with speeds above about 30,000 km/sec. (67 million miles/hr.) are introduced, these theories begin to break down. That is where Einstein's theories take over and offer a better explanation of how things work. This; however, does not mean that this is the end of our search for truth and that we now have the answers to all the questions in the physical universe as some scientists would like us to believe. It only means that we now have a slightly better understanding of how things work in our observable world than Newton did during his brief sojourn on Earth with the more limited resources he had available to him at the time. We are still considerably in the dark when it comes to explaining phenomenon outside of our own back yard. Every time a probe ventures to a distant planet, new discoveries are made and our understanding of what is really there and how it works is altered. What we thought was correct must be revised to fit the actual scenario. This concept that Einstein's theories, although more advanced than Newton's, not only apply to a better understanding of our Solar System, but to the entire Cosmos as well may, or may not, prove to be entirely accurate. The primarily result of this is that scientists frequently create incorrect theories about things they think they understand, but in reality do not. It is possible that in the future Einstein's hypotheses may require corrections to more accurately correspond to the workings of the actual Universe just as Einstein's more advanced theories revised Newton's perception of the natural world.

Some mathematicians use complex equations to attempt to validate their theories with predetermined conclusions. Nearly everyone has seen blackboards on TV or so called scientific papers covered with impressive equations that they are allegedly able to solve. These equations seldom contain any real numbers but numerous variables, usually represented by letters of the Greek alphabet, which are not defined. Supposedly what each of these unknown quantities represent is known by their colleagues. The problem with this idea is that a single equation cannot be solved if there is more than one unknown and a system of simultaneous equations can be solved for more than one variable only if there is the same quantity or fewer equations than unknowns. The problem arises when the equations are underdetermined or inconsistent, which is usually the case when trying to rationalize cosmic events. More often than not, the mathematician predefines many of the unknowns or considers them irrelevant and deletes them from the equations. This leads to unscientifically attained conclusions based on inaccurate original presuppositions. These equations are often so complex that super computers working at extremely high-speeds for significant lengths of time are required to solve them. Many of their rough calculations and results are predicated on the information obtained from these theoretical computer models. The computers are not the problem; they are usually quite accurate in their computations. It is the erroneous information that the mathematician inputs that is usually at fault.

Numerous mathematical equations either contain "infinity" in their calculations or results. It is the consensus by mathematicians that division by zero is impossible and not a valid computation, but they accept the use of infinity for convenience in their advanced mathematical endeavors as an abstract concept although division by zero mathematically equals infinity. Infinity is intrinsically impossible and can never be reached either mathematically or otherwise. If that were true, what is the value of infinity plus one? It becomes the new infinity and the old infinity becomes infinity minus one. This can be repeated indefinitely without reaching a compelling conclusion. What about infinity squared or infinity multiplied by infinity? There is no significance to anything being infinitely large or small since it would mean that nothing including the quantity of all the known and unknown elements in the Universe could ever exceed this number. This is not possible. Infinity is a philosophical concept that can never be attained. When a mathematician or a super-computer arrives at the conclusion that the answer is infinite, a mistake has been made with the inputted data, there is an error in the computations, or the result is so immense that it does not bare any resemblance to reality or it represents a theory that is incapable of describing a situation properly. Nothing in nature or our known Universe is infinitely large or infinitely small, that is a misnomer. Infinity is used successfully in mathematics or physics when applied to signify an unbounded limit but cannot be observed in reality.

There is a theory that states that if you go far enough in a straight line in the Universe you will eventually return to your point of origin. This theory postulates that the Universe is spherical in shape and lends credence to its being "infinite" since it means you never reach a boundary. It fails to indicate what lies outside of this boundless sphere. This concept may incorporate some legitimacy in a potential yet to be detected multi-dimensional Cosmos, but does not appear to stand up to scrutiny in our perceived three spatial and fourth temporal dimensional time-space continuum.

The unseen microscopic universe presents another problem that cannot be solved with our present technology and may never be fully understood for a number of reasons. We can only magnify small objects to a limited extent with microscopes that use visible light to form the observed enlarged image. The very best compound light microscope utilizing multiple lenses is capable of magnification up to 2,000 times due to physical limits imposed by the wavelength of the light. An electron microscope is capable of better magnification and resolution than one that makes use of light, since the wavelength of electrons is considerably shorter than that of photons of visible light. Electron microscopy is capable of magnification up to 10,000,000 times with greater resolution. Since an object is not visible under a microscope that is less than half the wavelength of its illumination source, a visible light microscope cannot detect viruses and molecules, but an electron microscope can. Atoms are too small to be seen with any degree of clarity even with an electron microscope, but they have been viewed.

The word "Atom" means indivisible or something that cannot be divided further, since only a short while ago, in the eighteenth century, this was perceived to be the smallest ultimate particle of matter. We now know that the atom is not the smallest particle of matter and that they are composed of protons, neutrons and electrons, with protons and neutrons composed of even smaller particles called quarks. These smaller particles cannot be seen even through an electron microscope, so scientists use a particle accelerator, such as the large Hadron Collider, to accelerate two high energy particle beams to near the speed of light in opposite directions and make them collide. Scientists believe that analysis of the byproducts of these collisions provide evidence of the structure of the subatomic world. These only become apparent at high energies for extremely short periods of time and therefore may be hard or impossible to study in other ways. Scientists have discovered what they call the Higgs Boson particle using this method of colliding high energy particle beams and seeing what gets knocked off. This is analogous to blind people crashing automobiles together at high speeds and then trying to determine what the cars looked like originally by studying the pieces that were knocked off during the collision.

Many scientists believe that we have reached the limit on subatomic particles. Not too long ago, they thought the atom was the smallest ultimate particle of matter. Now they believe these collider byproducts are. We may never be able to determine with certainty anything smaller than these particles that we cannot hope to see. How do we know that there are not even considerably smaller subatomic particles beyond our wildest imagination? How can we know for sure that we have even come close to discovering what small really is? We have redefined how large the known Universe is by an incredible amount; maybe someday we will discover just how small the smallest particle in the Universe really is. The physics relating to the macro-universe of the extremely large does not completely agree with the micro-universe of the extremely small. Advanced mathematical equations imply that when cosmological macro gravitational theories are applied on the micro scale, several hypotheses that explain an expanding Universe are inconsistent. To date, theoretical physicists have yet to combine the theory of general relativity with quantum mechanics by solving the problem of the quantization of gravity with the other three fundamental forces, electromagnetism and the strong and weak nuclear forces (fusion and fission).

"String Theory" is a relatively new theory that includes such concepts as superstrings, branes and additional dimensions and tries, so far without success, to create a fundamental link between general relativity and quantum physics. The goal is to create a "Theory of Everything", but so far they have been unsuccessful since these ideas are so far out in "left field" as to be almost comical. The scientific community has not arrived at any satisfactory consensus regarding the basic nature of quantum physics. There is not a shred of evidence, other than super computer generated mathematical absurdities, to confirm any of this. To a physicist, a string is one dimensional with only length and no width or depth. Not only is a single dimensional string impossible in nature, even a two-dimensional object is not possible in reality since even the flattest particles that atoms are composed of have depth. Even a shadow is not two dimensional, it has a third dimension between the surface that the shadow is cast upon and the object blocking the light know as the umbra. Although some things appear as one or two dimensional from the perspective of the human eye, in reality all objects on Earth, and in all probability in the Universe, exist in Euclidean Space that consists of three spatial dimensions. Any additional or lesser dimensions can only be visualized mathematically and are; therefore, hypothetical until proven otherwise.

Time may be considered as a fourth temporal dimension, but cannot be observed, only experienced. According to Einstein's Special Theory of Relativity, time is relative to the observer's frame of reference and the speed of light is constant for all observers. There is no universal time shared by everything, but on Earth, it appears that time is absolute because things are moving so slowly at ordinary every day speeds. This theory of time dilation states that time runs slower as speed increases until time comes to a stop at the speed of light. Clocks measure an interval or passage of time, but not time itself. Seconds, minutes, hours and days are artificial manmade units that measure time intervals based on Earthly observations. This clock time is based on the Earth's rotation with respect to the Sun, but is not relevant in outer space where stars and planets are of different sizes than Earth, rotate at different speeds and possess different gravitational attractions. Time appears to flow in one direction only, from past to present to future. We live in the present, can recall events in the past, but cannot return to the past, and we can perceive the future, but have no memory of it. Do we really know what time is? There is still a great deal of controversy amongst scientists and mathematicians as to whether time is real or just perceived.

4

SIGNIFICANT ERRORS IN THE BIG BANG THEORY, THE EXPANDING UNIVERSE & MACRO EVOLUTION

There are many things that are intrinsically wrong with the theory of the "Big Bang" that any real scientist, engineer, physicists or mathematician that chooses to look closer at the known facts could ascertain. Unfortunately, many do not have a desire to confirm their belief whatever the consequences or ridiculous nonsense they have to conjure up to arrive at their forgone conclusion. Advanced mathematics is a science of deductions where an individual assumes certain things and infers conclusions from them. Most of the complex answers to these theories are arrived at with the use of super computers. When incorrect assumptions are imputed, the conclusions arrived at are also flawed. As they say in computer science, "garbage in, garbage out" that implies that if inaccurate data is entered, no matter how refined an information system may be, the outcome will be misleading. Depending upon the information inputted, computer models can be made to corroborate nearly any desired conclusion.

During the time of Aristotle and Ptolemy, it was believed that the Earth was the center of the Universe and that the Sun, planets and stars revolved around it. Only a short while later, in the sixteenth century, Copernicus proposed that the Earth is not in a central position and that the Earth and other planets in our Solar System revolved around the Sun. Later, it was discovered that the entire Solar System is only a small part of our Milky Way Galaxy which was at one time thought to be our entire Universe. Now, the Hubble telescope has resulted in the theory that the Milky Way Galaxy is only one of countless billions of other galaxies in the Universe and our concept of the size of the entire Universe has expanded immensely. So why do these pseudo-scientists believe, without reservation, that they now have a complete understanding of the Universe and that they are now absolutely correct? They act as if they know with absolute certainty that the "Big Bang Theory" is not a theory, but absolute fact and cannot be reasonably challenged.

The Catholic priest and Belgian cosmologist, Georges Lemaitre, first introduced this concept that the Universe was created from a single particle that contained all the matter in the Universe which he described as the "primeval atom" in 1927. Sir Fred Hoyle, a British astrophysicist, coined the term "Big Bang" as a derogatory name for this theory that he never accepted; however, this moniker for the theory was accepted by many prominent scientists and the term "Big Bang Theory" is now widely acknowledged as conventional wisdom. The majority of scientists now accept the claim that the entire Universe started from a singularity that was infinitely small, hot and dense. Where this singularity came from and what caused it to expand and cause the entire Cosmos to exist as we see it today, nobody seems to know. It requires all known physics to have not existed prior to the "Big Bang" and only shortly thereafter to miraculously have appeared out of nothing. Historically, even in ancient Greek philosophy, there was this concept that "Nothing comes from nothing" that states that what exists now has always existed, meaning that no new matter can come into existence where there was none before. According to Einstein's famous equation derived from his Special Theory of Relativity, Energy = Mass x C^2 at constant momentum, where C = Speed of light in a vacuum. This equation shows explicitly how mass can be converted to energy and energy to mass and upholds the concept of conservation of mass. If this theory is true, neither matter nor energy can be created nor destroyed, only changed in form; hence, there could not be a singularity from which all matter and energy was formed. The "Big Bang" theory requires the creation of matter and energy from nothing which by definition is creationism. This would be a miracle, and many scientists don't believe in miracles.

Even if it is assumed that the "Big Bang" theory is in fact true, the mathematics involved to back up this allegation, do not work without considerable manipulation. In order to be mathematically valid, these astrophysicists admit that during the first fraction of a second of existence, the acceleration of the expansion of the Universe must be considerably faster than their theory allows for, so rather than revise their original hypothesis that they have already decided was correct, they introduced a fudge factor that they called "Cosmic Inflation". They say that during the first fleeting instant, space expanded in the early Universe at a much higher rate than the speed of light and then slowed and continued to expand at this slower rate. These scientists cannot explain what caused this initial inflation to occur when they say it did and what caused it to terminate at the appropriate time to give validity to their equations. This "Cosmic Inflation" theory can in no way be rationally justified, but had to be introduced to make their mathematical hypothesis work.

Another problem with the "Big Bang" theory is that, if accurate, our Universe appears to contain much more matter than can be accounted for in our visible stars. Time for another fudge factor to make the mathematics work! This time they term the missing mass "Dark Matter" although no one has ever seen or detected it. Supposedly "Dark Matter" consists of about 26.8% of our Universe while normal known matter consists of only 4.9%. That's a pretty large error! It's not looking good for their original "Big Bang" theory, but they don't stop there.

Finally, they say that our Universe is expanding faster than can be accounted for by the "Dark Matter" required by their bogus equations, so it is time for an additional fudge factor to make everything come out in favor of their original theory that they are unwilling to revise. The remaining 68.3% apparently consists of "Dark Energy". Nobody has ever detected any of this either! Now they have proven that the "Big Bang Theory" is correct and cannot be reasonably challenged. Really!

The biggest tragedy here is that they are teaching this rubbish in our schools so that our younger generation is being indoctrinated into believing this nonsense is factual without confirmation. Is their "Big Bang Theory" correct? Taking into account all the fudge factors required for legitimacy, it is exceedingly unlikely. Are people that look at all the adjustments made to lend credence to the original supposition really that naive as to believe there is an iota of truth in it? Scientists now say that they understand the 4% of the Universe that is made up of atoms, but that the remaining 96% that they don't understand is composed of dark matter and dark energy. It is doubtful that they even understand that much! It is time to abandon a theory that requires this much extraneous hypotheses for any kind of validity. Approximately 96% of the "Big Bang" theory is strictly unsubstantiated nonsense thought up by a few pseudo-scientists in search of fame and fortune. It is time to revise their original theory to one that does not rely on excessive manipulation of their mathematical equations to arrive at their conclusions.

Summarizing what is wrong with the Big Bang Theory: 1) All the known laws of physics could not have existed in the infinitely small, hot and dense singularity prior to the "Big Bang" 2) No one can explain where this singularity came from and what caused it to expand to create the entire Cosmos 3) If neither matter nor energy can be created nor destroyed, a singularity is not possible 4) The creation of matter and energy from nothing is the definition of creationism 5) The mathematics that supposedly back up this allegation require considerable manipulation 6) Cosmic inflation must be introduced to make the mathematical hypothesis work 7) Theoretical dark matter and dark energy are required to validate the "Big Bang" bogus equations 8) The "Big Bang" theory is entirely unsubstantiated.

For the "Big Bang" theory to have any chance at being valid the Universe must be expanding. Due to the immense distances between objects in interstellar space, there is no observable movement over such relatively short time spans. A short time span, in cosmological terms, frequently encompass considerably more than an individual's lifetime on Earth. Consequently, a significant part of the implied expansion of the Universe is accounted for by measurements made of the distances to far off spiral nebulae and Cepheid stars in the Cosmos. Because of the extreme distances from Earth, they cannot use any conventional methods to make measurements to extremely faraway objects. The conventional method used for measuring the distance to nearby stars is known as the stellar parallax method. The parallax method measures the angle of inclination between two sight lines observed approximately six months apart when the Earth is on opposite sides of the Sun. This results in the greatest distance possible for the third side of the triangle when making the measurement from Earth by triangulation. To determine considerably greater distances, they use what is known as the Hubble "Red Shift" in the light coming from these stars. They explain that there is a "Doppler Effect" in the light waves from these stars similar to the known Doppler Effect of sound waves here on Earth that can be measured and determines if the stars are moving away or approaching us and by how much. The definition of red shift is when light from an object is shifted towards the red end of the electromagnetic spectrum with a corresponding lower level of photon energy. This object is allegedly moving away from the observer. A blue shift supposedly indicates that the object has a higher level of photon energy and is moving towards the observer. Before this nonsense of cosmological red shift due to the expansion of the Universe became the latest rage, it was concluded that a star's color was an indication of its temperature, not its apparent motion towards or away from the observer. Essentially, colors range from red giant stars that are cooler to blue and white dwarfs that are the hottest. The temperature ranges and sizes of stars vary considerably. Our Sun which appears yellow has a surface temperature of about $5,800°$ Kelvin and falls somewhere in between these extremes.

The Doppler Effect, named after Christian Doppler who proposed it in 1842 in Prague, is caused by the apparent compression or expansion of sound waves through the Earth's atmosphere; the medium through which the sound waves are traveling. This effect applies to sound waves traveling through a known medium, in this case air, but not necessarily for light waves traveling through the vacuum of space. The light waves in space are not traveling through a medium; hence there cannot be any apparent compression or expansion of the light, or a corresponding "Red Shift" in a medium. Even if indeed the theory of "Red Shift" is valid, then a substantial number of galaxies should exhibit a "Blue Shift" as well. Allegedly, only about 100 galaxies in our immediate vicinity out of the purported billions of galaxies in the Cosmos exhibit a small blue shift. Since this means that nearly all stars must be traveling away from Earth, the Earth must be located at, or very near, the center of the Universe. That seems very unlikely! Additionally, these galactic red-shifts are observed to occur in discrete quantized levels and elliptical galaxies exhibit smaller red-shifts than spiral ones suggesting that the red-shift is not caused by expansion of the Universe as is the current consensus.

Although the deep vacuum of intergalactic space is a near perfect vacuum, it is not completely devoid of matter and contains a few hydrogen atoms per cubic yard. Due to the vast distances involved, whether or not this is true for all of space cannot be established with any certainty. At first glance, this doesn't seem like much, but due to the vastness of galactic space, the total mass of these hydrogen atoms exceeds the total mass of all observable matter in the Universe. Any debris such as cosmic dust; however, that star light must pass through before reaching the observers eyes may cause a red shift when photon energy is lost. This is known as the "Tired Light" theory. There is a newer alternative to the "Tired Light" theory known as the "Quantum Electrodynamics (QED)" theory that suggests that red-shift is caused by absorption of galaxy light in dust particles. The QED theory implies that the Universe is static in nature and not expanding as the Hubble red-shift theory suggests. This makes more sense as it does not require the existence of the principle of dark energy or dark matter that has never been substantiated. The Hubble Law is obviously flawed and there is no rationale to assume that the Cosmos is expanding. Furthermore, in order to be able to calculate the "Red-shift" of far away stars, the original brightness of the star must be known. According to these astrophysicists, they can peer millions and even billions of years into the past and determine with great accuracy what the original brightness was, based on observations of so called "known stars". Also, the assumption is made that the light has traveled millions, even billions, of light years without passing through any interstellar matter that may have altered the perceived speed of the light. This is pure nonsense!

Light has properties of both waves and invisible particle-like photons. Visual light only occupies a very small band (between 400 and 700 nanometers) of the total electromagnetic spectrum that has an enormous range of frequencies. In addition to visible light, the entire electromagnetic spectrum also contains longer wave infrared radiation, microwaves and radio waves as well as shorter ultraviolet, x-rays and gamma rays. None of these are visible to the human eye. The only way humans can detect any of these is through instrumentation that converts them to visible light or sound waves. Scientists still do not fully understand this dual nature of light, but they have no problem creating preposterous assumptions and passing them off as factual.

How do we know that the Earth is nearly five billion years old and that the Universe is about 13.8 billion years old? According to the pseudo-scientists, the ages of materials can be determined by radioactive dating of geological events. Geologists use what they refer to as absolute dating methods, also known as numerical dating, to determine an approximate age for rocks. This involves measuring the radioactive decay of isotopes of such materials as Potassium 40 and Uranium 238 and is based on the assumption that this radioactive decay of material has always proceeded at a constant rate. There is an inherent flaw in this method since no one was present to measure the radioactive elements of a rock when it was formed and it is; therefore, impossible to know what the original ratio of the basic element to the radioactive element was. Also, it is very likely that over the long duration of time involved that the sample could become contaminated. This is not an exact science and is based on assumptions about the past that are suspect. Geologists conjure up an assumed geological history depending on numbers that they get from the lab by measuring rates of sedimentary deposition and erosion based on the assumption that the rate of decay is constant. Geology, if a science at all, is heavily influenced by unproven and unreliable dogma and assumptions.

Carbon 14 dating is probably the most commonly used method for determining the age of bones and remnants of life forms. Radiocarbon dating consists of comparing the amount of normal carbon with the amount of the radioactive carbon 14 isotope that is found in a sample. Even the use of accelerator mass spectrometry to analyze the relative levels of carbon and radioactive carbon has resulted in flawed conclusions. It is not uncommon for different laboratories to establish significantly different ages for the same object! While some of this deviation could possibly be explained by contamination or erred methodology in the labs themselves, it is apparent that the problems with carbon dating are much more complex than that. Also, carbon dating cannot determine if something is a billion, or even a million years old; carbon dating is good for a maximum of about 40,000 years, if that. Carbon dating is based on two simple assumptions; that the amount of carbon 14 in the atmosphere and the rate of decay have always been constant. Current tests reveal that the amount of C-14 in the atmosphere has been increasing ever since first measured over 50 years ago and that this may be tied to the declining strength of the Earth's magnetic field or the amount of carbon available to organisms in the past. There are too many unknowns to allow the carbon dating process or any other process based on radioactive element decay cited by biased scientists to be as accurate as they assert. There appears to be new evidence that the previously held scientific belief that the rate of decay of Carbon 14 and other radioactive isotopes such as Uranium 238 is constant may not be true. This discovery challenges the accepted hypothesis on the age of the Earth as well as that of the entire Universe.

Regardless of whom you believe, nearly everybody agrees that, at most, humans have inhabited Earth for only a few thousand to tens of thousands of years. That is why they call most of the earliest time line prehistoric, since there is no reliable evidence to verify that anyone that old ever existed. We have history and can prove what happened only during this relatively short period in which events were recorded; about 6,000 years. Anything pertaining to events prior to that is pure speculation. To say that certain laws of physics were the same billions of years ago throughout the Universe as they are on Earth today can never be more than a theory and can never be proven as absolute fact as many respected scientists would have you believe. They may be correct, but anything that happened prior to man's presence on Earth is just speculation and cannot be proven since no one was there to observe and record it.

Recently, scientists claim that they have trained the Hubble telescope at a very small segment of space in the region of the constellation Ursa Major for an extended period of time. They allege that even in this region of space where they had previously observed little or no matter, they have discovered many galaxies billions of light years from Earth. If this is the case, it proves that their Big Bang Theory is incorrect, since it implies that there were fully formed galaxies existing billions of years ago very shortly after the creation of the Universe. The oldest known and most distant galaxy from Earth recently discovered by astronomers with the Hubble Space Telescope is supposedly about 13.4 billion light years away. Assuming this galaxy was created when the Universe was only about 400 million years old, the material from the "Big Bang" did not have time to coalesce into stars, much less form rotating galaxies. Astrophysicists claim that this galaxy is too bright and hot to have formed this early, but they still refuse to admit that their original hypotheses are wrong. They prefer to fabricate new beliefs to add credibility to their original conclusions about an expanding Universe. Their dogmatic beliefs will not be challenged in view of the facts.

In trying to resolve the age of the Universe, another thing to consider is whether the speed of light has always been constant or if it might have been considerably slower in the past than it is now. Although most scientists now agree that the speed of light is constant, they assume that during the first fraction of a second after the "Big Bang" there was this "Cosmic Inflation" where the speed of light was considerably faster. Their entire Big Bang Theory and the age of the Universe itself rely upon this unproven hypothesis. Bear in mind that they had to add this fudge factor to their equations to arrive at their predetermined conclusions. A considerably slower light speed in the past would shorten all the alleged distances in the Cosmos and reduce the perceived age of the Universe considerably. A light year is a distance measurement that would be much shorter if the speed of light was slower, resulting in shorter cosmic distances. Even if the speed of light is constant in a vacuum, that doesn't mean that it wasn't slowed considerably during earlier periods, prior to the formation of stars, when there was considerable cosmic dust present for the light beams to pass through prior to reaching Earth. It is a known fact that light travels slower through different common mediums such as water, air and glass. Recently light has been slowed from 186,282 miles/sec (in a vacuum) to a complete stop under laboratory conditions at Harvard University in a super-cooled cloud of gaseous sodium atoms by world-renowned physicist Dr. Lene Hau.

The claim that even our own Milky Way Galaxy is 100,000

light years across and is spiral in form may or may not be true. We are not observing the light from far distant stars in the same time frame as closer ones. If their time frame is correct, the light we see from more distant stars comes from much farther in the past than closer ones. The light from even the closest star outside of our solar system takes over four years to reach our eyes. Everything we see in space happened at different times in the past. Even the photons of light from the surface of our Sun take, on average, over eight minutes to reach Earth. So light that is now reaching our eyes here on Earth that came from the center of the Milky Way Galaxy, where they say an immense black hole resides, occurred approximately 30,000 years ago. If their concept of distance is correct, who can say with certainty that anything that we see in the Universe still exists in the present? If it does still exist, does it still appear as it did 30,000 years ago? A lot can change over a 30,000 year time span! Verification is not possible, only speculation, so anything that occurred significantly prior to recorded history can never be confirmed by mankind.

Just how big is the Hubble Space Telescope, or any Earth based telescope for that matter, to allow astronomers to peer so far back in time with such great accuracy. The Mount Palomar Earth based optical telescope mirror is only 200 inches in diameter and its image must be continually corrected to compensate for atmospheric conditions. While the Hubble Space Telescope does not have the disadvantage of an atmosphere to contend with, its mirror aperture is just under 95 inches in diameter. The cameras on the Hubble Space Telescope do not take color pictures, but only produce gray-scale pixels. Colors are added using filters, so any colored pictures have been artificially enhanced to provide an artful rendition. Considering the enormous distances involved, these telescopes don't provide anywhere near as much information as these astronomers would have us believe.

There have been immense advancements in our understanding of our world over just the last hundred years, but these changes can only be applied to the Earth and its inhabitants, not objects in outer space. There is a very good probability that the Earth is in fact part of a spiral galaxy as illustrated in media, but it is not a proven fact. No one has ever viewed it from afar. Only a cross section of one side of our "Milky Way" galaxy can be observed from our vantage point here on Earth, and the majority of it cannot even be seen. Man has five senses that he can utilize to view the world around him on Earth, but only one applies to the rest of the Universe, that of sight. Since man has never ventured further that 240,000 miles to the Moon and then only for brief periods in history, everything that is known about the remainder of the Universe has been made by deductive reasoning using eyesight alone. The only exceptions are materials from meteorites that have struck Earth and materials brought back from the surface of the Moon. The information that can be acquired from these small material samples is considerably limited in scope. Obviously, taste, feel and smell are unavailable to our celestial observations from Earth. Sound waves are mechanical in nature and need a medium to travel through, such as air or water, that doesn't exist in the vacuum of outer space, so that's out too. All of the information that can be received on Earth from objects in outer space is visual until someone actually goes there and experiences it firsthand. That is impossible now and very unlikely in the foreseeable future. It is true that heat from our Sun can be felt on Earth, but that is because it is only 93 million miles away, or one astronomical unit (AU); a very short distance in celestial terms. The next closest star to planet Earth, Proxima Centauri is slightly over four light years away (271,000 AU, or 25 trillion miles) and looks like a small dot when observed with the naked eye, or even through a small telescope, so no one can detect any heat from this star or any other with the exception of our Sun. In fact, Proxima Centauri cannot even be seen with the naked eye from Earth, since it is the smallest star in a triple star system known as Alpha Centauri. On Earth, we cannot distinguish each individual star with unaided eyesight alone; the three star system appears as one object even though the individual stars are separated from each other by considerable distances. The two larger stars, Alpha Centauri A and Alpha Centauri B is a binary system that orbits each other at a mean distance of 23 AU. The third star Alpha Centauri C (also known as Proxima Centauri); the closest star to Earth and our Sun is 13,000 AU from the Alpha Centauri A and B binary star system. To date, it is not known whether Proxima Centauri is actually bound to the binary star system of Alpha Centauri A and B.

Radio telescopes operate in the radio frequency portion of the electromagnetic spectrum that must be converted into sound waves to be heard and visual images to be viewed. A radio telescope of comparable magnification must be significantly larger than an optical telescope because the radio waves are considerably longer than visible light rays. They don't suffer from the problems inherent with optics in our atmosphere, but they must be isolated from electromagnetic sources here on Earth. Optical telescopes are located on mountain tops to receive as little atmospheric interference as possible, while radio telescopes are located in remote valleys to get away from the earthly electromagnetic interference. Until recently, the largest radio telescope in use was the Arecibo Observatory located in Puerto Rico with a 305 meter diameter single aperture spherical reflector. The largest single dish radio telescope on Earth recently constructed in China is the FAST (Five Hundred Meter Aperture Spherical Telescope) completed in September 2016 and is three times more sensitive than the Arecibo telescope.

Some creationists believe that the Universe is only 6,000 to 10,000 years old and most evolutionists believe it to be nearly 15 billion years old. That is quite a large discrepancy! Who is right? Scientific facts indicate that the truth may in reality be situated somewhere in between these two extremes; maybe not the nearly 15 billion years envisioned by the evolutionists, but probably considerably longer than the six to ten thousand years prophesied by the creationists. There are no credible records of man's prehistoric existence, but there are plausible data to authenticate prehistoric records of other life forms including dinosaurs. According to the Christian Bible Genesis creation account, God created the heavens and the Earth in six days and rested on the seventh. Many Christian scholars believe that each of these days are what we consider now to be 24 hours in length, or approximately the time required for the Earth to complete one full revolution on its axis. In the Genesis creation account, on the first day God made heaven and Earth. One major problem in assuming this first day was 24 hours long is the scientific fact that before the creation of Earth, there was no such thing as a 24 hour day. Taking into account Einstein's general theory of relativity, time is relative to the observer, and more specifically to the motion of that observer. Although the way we measure time is relative, time itself may be absolute. It is theorized that time slows as speed increases until at the speed of light, time comes to a complete stop. A 24 hour day is based on a time frame relative to Earth and prior to the Earth's creation that time frame did not exist. Another argument that is made by creationists concerns semantics based on what was written in holy books such as the Bible originally in Hebrew or other foreign languages that could be interpreted differently by different religious scholars. This unfortunately does not provide a scientific answer to the age of the Universe since, to begin with, not everyone believes in creationism. Unless the beliefs, theories, hypothesis or assumptions concerning the age of the Universe can be proven scientifically they are not based on the scientific method. To date no one has been able to confirm the age of the Universe with indisputable evidence or proof.

5

UNCONFIRMED EARTHLY PHENOMENON & MISGUIDED BELIEFS

There are numerous examples of articles in newspapers, periodicals or books, and on television that deal with earthly phenomenon that cannot be reasonably explained or that the authors of these works do not fully understand. In many instances, they provide the general public with unresearched or totally false narratives to either try to explain these things that they themselves do not understand, or they are just interested in providing a good story without accountability in the hope of financial gains. There are numerous deceptions that are considered to be truthful by many of the populace that do not understand the fundamental principles behind these claims that are not supported by documentary evidence.

There are daily television programs dealing with alien life and Earthly visitations. Why is it that with all the reports of sightings over hundreds and even thousands of years that have been supposedly documented, no one has ever been able to offer any authentic scientific proof of their existence? It does not seem logical that if there were all these visitations by extra-terrestrials over such a considerably long time frame that there would be no supportable proof of their presence other than unsubstantiated speculation.

If there is any validity in the claims of alien visitation in the past, in order to travel the vast distances necessary to visit Earth, their level of technology would have to be exceedingly more advanced than ours is even today. So, if this is the case, and early humans had access to this level of technology, why is there no evidence of it? We don't have any evidence of alien life either because contact is highly improbable given that there are so few and they are so isolated from one another, or because none are out there. Due to the vastness of the Cosmos and the potential for the existence of billions of galaxies, it is feasible and even probable that alien life does exists in some form somewhere, but that contact between alien life from other star systems is in all probability impossible due to the immense distances involved. Why is it that the only potential evidence of alien visitation from beings with far superior technology than humans are crude relics or structures that could have easily be crafted by people living on Earth at that time without the need for extraterrestrial assistance? The crude cave drawings and symbols left behind by ancient man even only a few thousand years ago are obviously not the work of superior beings from another planet outside our Solar System. Also, some "Ancient Alien Theorists" as they like to be called, believe that aliens have come here to destroy the human race. If this were the case, all human life would have been exterminated long ago. For aliens to have the knowledge to get here in the first place, they would have to be so far advanced beyond our wildest dreams as to make short work of destroying all human life without difficulty if they so chose.

Additionally, why would such technically advanced beings want to travel such long distances to visit technically inferior beings on a small insignificant planet in a remote region of the

Milky Way Galaxy? Could aliens have visited Earth in the past and could they be here now? It might be possible, but to date, there is no credible evidence that any such visitations have occurred. Due to the immense number of stars in our Milky Way Galaxy and the probable number of planets, it is very likely that a few of these planets have at least some of the many distinctive features found on Earth that allow life to exist. That; however, does not imply that these biological life forms would necessarily be carbon based or that they would be capable of communicating with humans or surviving in our oxygen rich environment. Because of the vastness of space and the extreme distances involved, it is unlikely that any intelligent beings have ever traveled to Earth or even know that we exist.

The famous "Blue Dot" photograph of the Earth taken in 1990 by the Voyager 1 space probe was taken from a distance of 3.7 billion miles. Even at that short a distance, astronomically speaking, the apparent size of the Earth was less than one pixel. Time lapse photography was employed to capture enough light and the image had to be magnified five times to be able to even see it. No features were visible from that distance. In fact, from even as short a distance from Earth as the Moon (240,000 miles), features as large as the major land masses and continents cannot be readily ascertained, much less any man-made objects. This was verified by observation and photographs of Earth taken from the Moon by astronauts. It does not appear likely that any alien could infer that there was any reason for them to visit such an insignificant planet in a star system so remote from their location wherever they originated from. There are no planets in our solar system, other than Earth, that are capable of supporting intelligent life forms and the nearest star system to us that is also unlikely to support advanced alien life is considerably farther away than the 3.7 billion miles that the photograph was taken from. It is particularly unlikely that any aliens have traveled to Earth from distant galaxies, much less our own, due to the immense expanse of space separating galaxies and the insignificance and location of our planet within our own galaxy. The SETI (Search for Extraterrestrial Intelligence) Institute has been searching the Universe for over 60 years utilizing radio telescopes, but to date have not had any success in discovering life beyond our planet, Earth. In the 60 years that SETI has been searching, a radio signal traveling at the speed of light could only reach an alien planet 30 light years distant and have them send back a signal that could be received on Earth within this time frame.

There are numerous television series or programs that claim without compelling evidence that all life originated outside our Solar System. They claim that life came to Earth either contained within a meteor or that it was brought here by alien beings. What they can't explain is that if life was procreated in outer space and came here on a meteor, where did it originate, how did it hitch a ride on a meteor, what impetus determined its unlikely path to Earth and how did it survived the trip intact? It would have taken an extremely long time to transverse the immense interstellar distance between any other locations capable of supporting life and Earth under incredibly inhospitable conditions. The probability of it arriving at this particular destination or any other location suitable to sustain life unscathed is unbelievably low; if it didn't succumb from the long duration trip in the extremely low temperature of outer space with lack of nourishment, how could it survive the intense heat of entry into the Earth's atmosphere? If life was brought to Earth by highly advanced alien beings, what was their incentive to come here and where are they now? Assuming that life on Earth was established by one of these implausible means, a significant question still remains unanswered. Where did life on this obscure planet outside our

Solar System originate? It still either had to come into existence without any outside help as envisioned in the "Big Bang Theory" by evolutionists, or by intervention by a superior being or identity, regardless of where it came from. The conditions on Earth, as far as we know, are the best to support and promote life as we know it in the known Universe. So where is the logic in supposing that life originated elsewhere and somehow was transported to Earth?

Some of these so-called "Ancient Alien Theorists" claim that they have evidence that certain aliens came from a region in a particular constellation, but there is a major flaw in this hypothesis. Constellations are not real; they are just figments of ancient philosopher's vivid imaginations that attempt to represent mythological creatures or gods in the celestial sphere to aid in navigation from the night sky. The stars that comprise most of these constellations appear in a single plane when viewed directly from Earth, but in reality, the stars that comprise these contrived constellations usually are a considerable distance from one another when viewed from a different perspective. For instance, at a right angle from the normal viewing direction, none of these fabricated constellations would be recognizable as such. It would be impossible to ascertain what general area any potential aliens might have come from, since often the stars that make up a particular constellation are in reality hundreds or thousands of light years distant from each other.

Granted, there appear to be many sightings of UFO's that defy explanation, but UFO stands for "Unidentified Flying Object", not alien spacecraft. Ninety five percent of all UFO sightings can be explained by known phenomenon while the remaining five percent may be from other earthly sources that we are not yet familiar with. For example, only a short while ago we were not even aware of "Sprites" that are electrical discharges in the upper atmosphere that defy logic. How many other occurrences that contradict reason such as ball lightning do we still not understand that may explain some of these incidents? Crop circles are another phenomenon that, to date cannot be explained. In this case; however, unlike many of the other unexplained phenomenon, we have tangible evidence of their existence. Granted, many of the simpler designs have been proven to be fakes, but there are considerably more highly sophisticated ones that defy reason and could not be constructed so complicated and with such precision in the time frame necessary to be man-made. This doesn't; however, prove that they were made by aliens, but only that we do not understand by whom or for what reason they are being created. There are many unexplained phenomenon that have yet to be resolved scientifically without resorting to the assumption that they had to be produced by an alien race of superior beings.

Another subject that is getting considerable attention from the media is the presumed existence of a creature know as "Bigfoot", "Yeti", "Sasquatch", or the "Abominable Snowman". Although there are reports of sightings from many people from numerous countries around the world that appear to be legitimate, no one has ever been able to provide one tangible shred of evidence of their existence. If in fact these creatures were real, with our present technology wouldn't someone have been able by now to do more than provide us with a suspicious hair sample, foot print or a blurred photograph? If they existed for as long a period as they claim, wouldn't there be evidence of some remains, or at least, their excrement? To date, no credible evidence has been found. The daily television programs that deal with searches for "Bigfoot" never actually provide any evidence of their existence, only conjecture. If they actually were able to prove their existence, that would end the television series and their revenue stream, so that is unlikely to happen in the foreseeable future. Is it possible that they actually exist? Yes, but it is unlikely. If they do exist, our scientists, with all their sophisticated equipment, that are spending countless hours looking for them are proving to be highly incompetent.

It seems reasonable to most people that it would take millions or even billions of years for changes in the Earth's crust, from the theoretical super-continent Pangaea, to separate into individual continents separated by thousands of miles. The problem with this is that Pangaea is only another unproven theory. The theory looks plausible based on the shapes of the continents that we see today and other factors, but it has never been verified as fact. One of the problems with this theory is that many of the continental shelves do not align with the edges of the continents. For the continents to drift apart there would need to be fracture points that correspond with the outlines of the continents. This theory can never be proven, since as the scientists themselves admit, no one was alive that long ago to verify it. Recently the theory of Continental Drift, that all the present day continents were originally a single continent has been rejected by most scientists. The newest theory of Plate Tectonics that replaces it is also a theory and nothing more and even the supporters of this hypothesis cannot agree upon how the plates move or what forces cause this movement.

It used to be that television programs dealing with evolution, alien life and other unconfirmed phenomena such as Bigfoot, were labeled "Science Fiction" since this is what they actually are. Now, every day there are numerous programs on television that discuss evolution and aliens as if they are real proven facts and label these programs as "Science", when in fact, there is no evidence of such. They convince their audiences that these things are factual with elaborate computer generated effects although they are not real and they do not actually have any substantial proof to back up their assertions. There have been so many technological and scientific advances in the past 100 years that many believe that we had to have had help from extra-terrestrial beings to achieve them. This could be true, but it is extremely unlikely, and there is no evidence that supports this theory. Apparently these people do not have much faith in mankind's ability to make technological and scientific advancements without outside assistance.

There are a substantial number of theories that are being postulated today with little or no scientific reasoning to back up these claims. One of these is the existence of the Kuiper Belt which is alleged to consist of a disc comprised of small Solar System bodies ranging in size from small chunks of ice to over 100 kilometers in diameter at a distance of 30 to 55 AU (2.8 to 5.1 billion miles) from the Sun. Although it has been confirmed that some smaller planetary bodies do exist at this distance from the Sun, such as the dwarf planets Pluto, Eris, and Makemake, the existence of an entire Kuiper Belt has never been proven or even observed. Eris, slightly larger than Pluto, actually exists slightly beyond the conjectural Kuiper Belt at about 68 AU (6.3 billion miles) from the Sun. Another supposition is the existence of the Oort Cloud that is purported to be a spherical band of icy objects that lies well beyond the Kuiper Belt. Unlike the Kuiper Belt, the Oort Cloud is claimed to exist in spherical form that completely encompasses the Solar System beginning at a distance of around 2,000 AU (186 billion miles) and extending out to about one light year from the Sun. Although the Oort Cloud is supposedly composed of two trillion objects, no one has ever seen it or been able to even provide a shred of evidence to confirm its existence. This is all hypothetical nonsense with no basis in fact.

Numerous astronomers, astrophysicists and astro-mathematicians that deal with astronomy, astrophysics and cosmology sometimes find it impossible to correlate their super-computer results with actual observations concerning the movement of planets, stars or other celestial bodies that exist in space. Rather than question or attempt to modify their erroneous results, they come up with all kinds of fabricated nonsense to validate their incorrect conclusions. These include the purported existence of Planet X or Planet 9 and a twin star to our Sun. Planet X was inferred to be responsible for discrepancies in the orbital motions of the outer planets Uranus and Neptune. All the known planets in our Solar System travel on slightly elliptical orbits that are nearly circular. According to a planetary scientist from NASA, Planet X is a hypothetical rogue planet that orbits the Sun on a highly elongated orbit that extends beyond Neptune. The planet is estimated to be four times the size of Earth with ten times the mass on an orbit around the Sun that takes 20,000 Earth years to complete. This planet is also known as Planet 9; the "9" indicating that it is the ninth planet in the Solar System and "X" because it is based on a prediction generated from super-computer simulation and detailed mathematical modeling and not direct observation. It was more recently discovered from more accurate measurements of the outer planets motions and mass that the planets are in fact moving as would be expected without the necessity for Planet X. Some professed conspiracy theorists, Christian numerologists and internet doomsday groups claim a Planet X they have named Nibiru is a wandering planet that will soon pass by or collide with Earth causing devastation from earthquakes, tsunamis and volcanic eruptions. They maintain that this planet is mentioned in the Christian Bible in the book of Revelation and will cause an apocalypse. This is just another example of the facts being altered to arrive at a predetermined conclusion. If indeed, this rogue planet X had orbited the Sun even in the distant past, greater than 20,000 years ago, it would have caused a disruption in the nearly circular orbits of the known planets that would be evident today. There is none because Planet

X is the figment of someone's vivid imagination being perpetrated by many with the same ostentatious ideas. There is another hypothetical allegation proposed by astronomers that our Sun is part of a long cycle binary star system with a dwarf brown or red star companion they call Nemesis that is alleged to have caused mass extinctions on Earth in the past. Nemesis is purportedly orbiting the Sun at a semi-major axis distance of about 1-1/2 light years and even though we have the infrared technology necessary to detect such objects none have ever been discovered. This is in all likelihood just more unscientific nonsense!

Another misconception that is being perpetuated in many movies and TV programs that is not accurate is the exploding fuel tanks on automobiles and aircraft, and at fueling stations. In many instances automobiles are shown to explode upon contact with other objects; in some cases an automobile launches off a cliff and explodes before even making contact with the ground. Sometimes, there are multiple explosions resulting from the same event. Gas pumps are shown to explode violently when ruptured. These illustrations are of course faked but have convinced many viewers to believe that some fuels such as gasoline, diesel fuel and aviation jet fuels are highly explosive. This is a totally false assumption. The fuel tank is usually located in the rear of a vehicle and is not apt to be ruptured in the event of an accident. In reality, outside of Hollywood, fuel tanks never explode! If gasoline were in fact highly explosive such as TNT, it would not be suitable for use as a fuel in an internal combustion engine. The minimum flame speed that distinguishes detonation from deflagration is 1,000 meters per second which is supersonic and produces a shock wave. As an example, the detonation velocity of TNT (Trinitrotoluene) is about 6,940 meters per second while the stoichiometric flame speed of gasoline in a combustible mixture of air is only 0.34 meters per second (deflagration at subsonic speed) which means that TNT results in an explosive velocity that is over 20,000 times greater than the gasoline's flame speed. TNT explodes; gasoline burns rapidly, but does not explode per se. An explosion is defined as "detonation that propagates supersonically through shock waves" while deflagration consists of "combustion through heat transfer". Low flame propagation velocity events such as gunpowder deflagrations are often referred to as "explosions" although technically they propagate at subsonic velocities. Gasoline, diesel, alcohol or jet fuel will not even burn in an enclosed fuel tank. Three things are required for combustion; the fuel itself, a spark of sufficient strength and the correct amount of air to create the proper fuel/air mixture. The stoichiometric ratio of fuel to air is the ideal ratio for complete combustion. The stoichiometric ratio for gasoline is about 14.7:1, or 14.7 parts of air required for one part gasoline. This ratio is 15.6:1 for Jet A-1 (kerosene), 14.5:1 for diesel, 6.4:1 for alcohol, and 1.7:1 for nitromethane. In reality, in an automobile's spark ignition internal combustion engine the stoichiometric ratio is not ideal for all conditions, but must be varied within a range to allow for numerous variable conditions such as maximum power or maximum economy to obtain the best driving conditions. Nowadays this is done very effectively through the use of electronic controls. The fuel will burn with either more or less than the ideal fuel/air ratio within limits although less efficient. For gasoline, the combustible fuel/air ratios, or flammability limits, are approximately 8:1 to 18.5:1. Beyond these limits combustion is not possible even if a suitable source of ignition is present. Additionally, if a suitable spark is not present combustion is not possible. As often portrayed in the cinema, someone throws a lit cigarette into a pool of gasoline and it either bursts into flame or explodes. In reality, a lit cigarette does not provide an adequate source of ignition and will, in fact, be extinguished by the fuel. A diesel fueled engine may use a glow plug as a heating aid during initial startup, but relies on a high compression ratio to increase the temperature adequately to provide compression ignition and sustain combustion without a spark plug during normal operation. The fuel storage tanks at filling stations are located below ground and do not pose a threat from explosion or even fire since there is not sufficient air available for combustion to occur, nor is there any suitable source of ignition. The above ground pumps are equipped with mechanical and electrical protection measures and safety shutoff devices that turn off the pumps if they are breached by a vehicle hitting them or if the fuel lines are ruptured for any reason. This leaves only a relatively small amount of fuel that may be spilled during a mishap that is capable of causing a fire, but not detonation.

When a jet airliner crashes the outcome is usually devastating, not because of an explosion, but because of extenuating circumstances. Usually the airplane hits the ground at a high rate of speed and the fuel tanks are ruptured catastrophically creating a formidable vapor cloud. The resulting fireball is due to the substantial amount of fuel carried onboard in comparison to the amount carried in an automobile fuel tank and the hot gas turbine engines provide a readily available source of ignition.

Recently a deranged individual committed mass murder in Las Vegas when he fired automatic weapons into a crowd below from high-rise hotel building windows. It was reported that he also fired a high powered rifle at a jet fuel storage tank at McCarran International Airport. The media reported that there were signs of bullets hitting one of the tanks, but not penetrating it. They avowed that if the tank wall was breached a massive explosion would have devastated the entire area and caused considerably more damage and loss of life. Massive above ground jet fuel storage tanks are not susceptible to explosion or even burning if their wall is breached by a bullet. Does anyone actually believe that these tanks would be located in a highly populated area if this were possible? Apparently so! First off, if a bullet did penetrate the tank it not only would not cause an explosion, it wouldn't even start a fire. These tanks are usually double-walled so it would possibly cause a small leak if it penetrated both the outer and inner walls. Many of these fuel storage tanks also have floating roofs to diminish the volume of vapor in the tank as the liquid fuel is consumed. Unlike gasoline, jet fuel is mostly kerosene with a high vapor pressure so it does not form much vapor anyway and it's the vapor that burns, not the liquid. Additionally, the flash point is over 100° Fahrenheit, considerably higher than gasoline, so if someone dropped a lit match into a puddle of the fuel it would in all probability extinguish the flame, not start a fire. Jet fuel burns hotter than gasoline once inflamed, but is much harder to ignite in the first place due to its considerably higher vapor pressure and flash point.

Another misconception is that a natural gas (mostly methane) leak into air in an enclosed area will result in an explosive detonation if a suitable source of ignition is introduced. Frequently houses being leveled by gas "explosions" often with ensuing deaths are given as examples to prove this theory. In reality, the laminar flame speed of natural gas in a combustible mixture of air varies over a narrow range, but averages 0.40 meters per second which is not adequate to trigger an explosion per se, only deflagration since it is well below the minimum speed of 1,000 meters per second required to produce detonation that results in a supersonic shock wave. Deflagrations primarily occur at laminar flame speeds below 100 meters per second and usually at considerably lower velocities. Proponents of this "gas explosion" theory state that detonation must have occurred due to the extreme destruction and often complete leveling of the structure.

In reality, the structure is severely damaged from over-pressure that can blow out doors and windows, result in death, and level a poorly constructed building. An actual detonation explosion would cause considerably more damage from flying shrapnel and the accompanying shock wave, shattering or pulverizing items in its path. Although natural gas consists primarily of methane, often with added ethane and propane, in some parts of the world the composition of the natural gas contains large amounts of heavier hydrocarbons that can increase the laminar flame speed considerably resulting in more severe damage when ignited in an enclosed space, but still not enough to constitute a detonation explosion.

There is an idiom that says that "If it looks like a duck, swims like a duck, and quacks like a duck, then it probably is a duck". This expression does not: however, typically apply to what often appears to be an explosion. Just because something is ignited and is extremely hot, expands rapidly with often devastating results and on occasion sounds like an explosion, in most cases the laminar flame speed is too low and the event is in all probability a deflagration, not an actual detonation explosion.

Many people are predisposed to accept as true what they want to believe despite the facts that contradict their beliefs. There are those that attempt to substantiate their beliefs based on anecdotal evidence or limited personal experiences to justify an argument. There are many conspiracy theories involving such subjects as politics, science, religion, climate change and extraterrestrials that are fabricated without any definitive confirmation in an effort to try to explicate an unknown phenomenon that does not appear to have a compelling explanation. The majority of the world's population does not have a scientific background and these fictitious rationalizations give them a sense of control over a situation that they do not fully understand and that consequently

71

makes them feel threatened. Some secret societies such as the Freemasons, Illuminati, Knights Templar, Rosicrucian, Knights of Malta, Jesuits, and the SETI Institute among numerous others perpetuate these erroneous suppositions.

The Bavarian Illuminati was a secret society originally established in 1776 by Adam Weishaupt in Germany to overthrow the Bavarian monarchy and the religious influence over public life of the state religion, Roman Catholicism. Although there are modern societies that use the "Illuminati" moniker, there is no evidence that the original Bavarian Illuminati survived beyond its suppression in 1785. More recently, a number of fraternal organizations have emerged that claim to descend from the original Bavarian Illuminati, but there is no apparent evidence of any legitimacy to this proclamation. Conspiracy theorists credit Illuminati agendas as their primary focus for all imaginable catastrophes, anomalies and causes of economic decline.

One of the more familiar conspiracy theories involves the argument that the water vapor condensate trailing aircraft engines on jets flying at high altitudes often consist of chemical agents sprayed into the exhaust by government agencies to alter climate patterns. They often refer to photographs of vapor trails that are orange in color as proof of their postulation. In reality, the reason the condensed water vapor trails sometimes appear orange is due to the Sun being below ten degrees above the horizon when they are observed. Under this condition, the Sun's rays are nearly horizontal and pass through considerably more atmosphere than from the midday Sun resulting in greater atmospheric refraction. The small dust particles, water droplets and pollution scatter and absorb short wavelength light in the blue and green range and concentrate the longer wavelength red and yellow light resulting in the vapor trails appearing orange, the same as is observed when the longer red and yellow light rays are prevalent during a sunrise or sunset. During the Vietnam War, the U.S. military conducted Operation Popeye that experimented with weather modification. Cloud seeding with lead and silver iodide particles was deployed from aircraft in an attempt to extend the monsoon season, but this was only practical over a very limited proximity. The ability to make extensive changes to the world's climate is totally impractical due to the immense area of the Earth's surface in relation to the minuscule capacity of each aircraft and the number of aircraft that would be required to accomplish this undertaking being insurmountable.

Another conspiracy theory perpetuated by Dr. Judy Wood concerns the collapse of the twin World Trade Center towers in New York City after being rammed by jet aircraft in a terrorist attack on September 11, 2001 that involved two of four hijacked commercial jet aircraft. Dr. Wood's background is primarily in civil engineering with emphasis on stress analysis and strength of materials. Her theory that the twin towers did not collapse as reported by the media, but turned to dust from a directed energy weapon is not supported by fact. Support for her hypothesis relies on such unreliable evidence as videos, eyewitness statements, planted evidence and uninvestigated phenomenon. She concludes that the "directed energy weapon" used was muon-catalyzed fusion, a process that allows for nuclear fusion to transpire at near room temperature and pressure even though there are no accepted verifiable laws of physics that would permit cold fusion to occur. There are presently four known forms of energy, in order of magnitude from weakest to strongest; gravity, electromagnetism, weak nuclear force (fission) and strong nuclear force (fusion). Fission involves the breaking apart of atoms of uranium or plutonium and is what occurs in a nuclear power plant reactor or when an atomic weapon is detonated. Fusion is an attractive force between protons and neutrons that holds the nucleus together.

To create energy from a thermonuclear fusion reaction extreme pressure and temperatures of over four million degrees Kelvin, similar to what is generated within stars is required. For example, an atomic (fission) bomb is required to ignite the nuclear fusion of a hydrogen bomb. Cold fusion has only been accomplished on an extremely small scale under laboratory conditions, and even then the results are suspect. One of the problems inherent with cold fusion is that it requires several times more energy to produce than what is generated. Another problem is that muons are incredibly unstable and cannot be created in the quantities required to provide a practical source of energy. Isn't it reasonable to assume that if cold fusion were a practical means of generating cheap, clean abundant energy that energy companies worldwide would be clamoring to find a practical solution?

There is a conspiracy theory that involves the Alaska based research facility known as the High Frequency Active Auroral Research Program (HAARP). The purpose of this U.S. Air Force facility is to study the properties of the upper atmosphere to gain a better understanding of the ionosphere's response to continual natural stimulation by the Sun. The Ionospheric Research Instrument (IRI) employed is a passive high power radio frequency transmitter used to temporarily stimulate a narrow region of the ionosphere to obtain pertinent data. It is alleged by conspiracy theorists that the real purpose of this scientific endeavor is to use directed energy to control the weather as well as other nefarious activities such as provoking earthquakes, floods, droughts and tornadoes or producing electromagnetic weapons. The problem with this assumption is that the IRI transmitter is just 72 feet high and covers an area of less than 31 acres; insignificant in comparison to the 126 billion acre surface area of the Earth. It is not possible that sufficient energy could be generated from such a small facility to even remotely affect the ionosphere in a significant way, or affect the upper atmosphere at a much greater distance than overhead of the IRI transmitter array. By way of illustration, the height of the troposphere where the Earth's weather occurs and the majority of the atmosphere is located is about seven miles thick with the stratosphere extending up to about 29 miles above the Earth's surface. If the Earth's 8,000 mile diameter is compared to the diameter of an average sized apple, the thickness of the Earth's atmosphere is analogous to the thickness of the apple's skin. The U.S. Air Force notified Congress of its intent to shut down the HAARP facility in 2014, later transferred ownership to the University of Alaska Fairbanks in August 2015 and was scheduled to resume operation sometime in 2017. If this was such an important research facility involved in the development of substantiated disreputable activities by the U.S. military, why would they do this? All these HAARP conspiracy theories are nonsense with no basis in scientific reality mostly perpetuated by individuals without an understanding or technical background in the subject material.

Obviously, there are some instances where conspiracies do take place, probably more prevalent in politics or religion than science, but the majority of these so called conspiracies are not credible. As the philosophical principal known as Occam's razor professes, "the more assumptions required to arrive at a consensus, the more likely the conclusion is false". The simplest explanation, although not always, is usually the most reliable.

6

THE GLOBAL WARMING HOAX &
THE OZONE HOLE DECEPTION

The so called "Green House" effect that is supposed to be causing global warming due to man's increased burning of fossil fuels is nothing more than a hoax perpetrated by greedy politicians and pseudo-scientists for their own personal monetary gain or out of sheer ignorance. Their agenda is clear; there are billions of dollars to be made in carbon credits for reducing carbon emissions and offsets that allow companies with large carbon footprints to continue to release carbon into the atmosphere for a price. This doesn't reduce the amount of carbon being released, but only makes those selling the credits and offsets richer. Recently, in their own words, these climatologists disclosed that spending trillions of dollars to reduce carbon dioxide emissions would only result in a 0.3° Celsius drop in the Earth's overall temperature over an 85 year period. Does it make sense for the United States Government to spend nearly 100 trillion dollars, with considerable economic consequences in an attempt to reduce the temperature of the Earth by a fraction of a degree? Of course not! Do these "scientists" even realize that the total area of the United States is less than 2% of the entire area of the world or that the United States only contributes about 15% of anthropogenic CO_2 emissions while the remaining world countries generate the remaining 85%? How would it even be possible when the population of the United States is about 330 million, or only around 5% of the total world's population? It is very unlikely that considerably larger countries like China or India and other third-world countries with little resources would be able or even willing to participate in this endeavor, not that this would make a significant difference even if they did. This is total nonsense and a waste of money that will not have any effect on the world's climate. It will only squander funds that could have been used more wisely.

More recently, extremists are trying to convince the populace that if we don't take immediate radical action to reverse man's contribution to global warming we will be facing an alarming catastrophic disaster that will result in total irreversible destruction of our entire planet within twelve years. These extremists tell us that we need to heed the advice of this majority of scientists and take radical action immediately or face dire consequences, but they fail to mention that these same scientists also declared that it is already too late. Remember that they said this extreme action would only decrease the world's overall temperature by about 0.3 degrees Celsius by 85 years from now. So, if they are correct, it is already too late and we are all doomed! It is a good thing that in reality they are wrong. There is nothing to worry about and no corrective action is required or even possible!

Governments literally spend billions of dollars on grants to scientists to prove that humans are causing global warming on an unprecedented scale. If they tell the truth and deny that this is the case, they are out of a job, so they lie and falsify results. Advocates of climate change maintain that the question of global warming has been established scientifically when in actuality, these so called "scientific" claims regarding climate cannot be backed up with verifiable facts. Very few of these scientists will admit that it is estimated that approximately 70% of all climate studies cannot be reproduced. It is reported that about 97% of "actively publishing climate scientists" taking a position on the subject of global warming agree with the consensus position that global warming is happening and that it is primarily being caused by human activity. So where did this 97% figure come from anyway? It is predominately contributed to John Cook who runs a website entitled "skepticalscience.com" that defends catastrophic anthropogenic global warming by misrepresenting the facts to further his misguided beliefs. Numerous politicians, media, and other "believers" embraced this charade, so today it is considered fact by far too many that have not taken the time to question this erroneous statement. This position is taken largely due to peer pressure on scientists to concede based on fear of ridicule or harassment by others or even loss of their career by PhD's with big ego's that refuse to admit their erroneous conclusions or the fear of research grants being rescinded and university tenure being revoked. More often than not, the public without question will side on the majority being right. There is no valid scientific evidence to back up the claim that global warming is factual or that it is being caused by man's burning of fossil fuels. In the United States, 31,000 scientists signed a petition declaring that anthropogenic global warming is not a serious concern and that an increase in CO_2 in the Earth's atmosphere would be beneficial to plant life and not result in runaway global warming. Although a signed petition does nothing to prove a scientific theory one way or the other, it does show that undoubtedly not every scientist agrees with those that declare man is contributing to global warming or that it is a serious threat to mankind. In 2011 President Barack Obama allocated over 2-1/2 billion dollars to "Global Warming" research with no funds committed to the actual scientific study of climate change. Just like his predecessor and staunch supporter of global warming Al Gore, without any scientific training or knowledge, his mind had already been made up that global warming was real and was man-made and as a politician he was determined to force his erroneous views on global warming on his constituents. Actually, they don't call it "Global Warming" anymore. They have changed the title to "Climate Change" since the idea of global warming perpetuated by the 2006 documentary film "An Inconvenient Truth" about former Vice-President Al Gore's campaign to convince people of a runaway global temperature increase caused by human intervention has since been shown not to be factual. There are a number of instances where Mr. Gore's claims contain scientific inaccuracies and political propaganda that is distinctly alarmist. His claim that global warming will cause a complete shutdown of the Meridional Overturning Circulation is highly unlikely and would not be possible in the short time frame he is proclaiming. He credited the disappearance of snow on Mt. Kilimanjaro and the drying up of Lake Chad to global warming but although it may be attributed to human intervention; there is insufficient evidence that this is the result of climate change. It is more likely due to other factors such as over-grazing, increases in population and regional climate discrepancies. There is insufficient evidence to show that hurricane Katrina or any other wind event is the result of global warming as he contends. His claim that polar bears are drowning due to exhaustion after swimming long distances is false. Polar bears are strong swimmers and regularly swim up to 50 miles or more. The only reliable recorded incident of polar bears drowning is one where four bears drowned in a storm. His claim that coral reefs are dying worldwide due to their inability to adapt to stress initiated by water temperature increases is not supported by science. There is reason to suspect that pollution and over-fishing may be more likely contributors to the demise of the coral. His assertion that predicts a sea-level rise of seven meters or more in the near future due to melting of the ice caps in Greenland and Antarctic is preposterous and not scientifically possible. According to Mr. Gore's claim, the North Polar ice cap should have disappeared before the year 2013, but it is still here! Maybe the motivation for this claim by a politician with little or no scientific training was the hundreds of millions of dollars that he made perpetuating this hoax, or maybe it was the 2007 Noble Peace Prize he shared for this "outstanding discovery". In his book on global warming Gore writes "Each one of us is a cause of global warming, but each of us can become part of the solution: in the decisions we make on what we buy, the amount of electricity we use, the cars we drive, and how we live our lives. We can even make choices to bring our individual carbon emissions to zero." In reality, for someone who is so concerned about "Global Warming", Mr. Gore's lavish lifestyle creates a considerably larger "Carbon Footprint" than most of the populace. The carbon footprint for his 10,000 square foot, twenty room mansion is over twenty times that of the average American's home and his three homes and lavish lifestyle consumes about 34 times as much energy annually as the average family. He has solar panels, but they only account for about 6% of his total energy consumption. He is usually chauffeured in a massive limousine, seldom in a more efficient vehicle and flies in a private plane rather than in a more eco-friendly commercial jet. In other words, like most corrupt politicians decree "Do as I say, not as I do". Mr. Gore would have you believe that in reality, he is living a "carbon neutral" existence since he purchases carbon credits that allegedly offset his excess consumption. What he fails to mention is that the company (Generation Investment Management) that he buys these credits from is partially owned and presided over by him. Furthermore, the energy and climate policies that Mr. Gore is urging Congress to adopt will financially benefit him immensely. Does this sound hypocritical? Most of the people marching in the streets with their banners denouncing man's involvement in causing planet destroying climate change are just echoing what they hear in the media and from politicians without any real understanding of the subject they are so fervently against. By far, the majority of these people have never bothered to research into whether there is any validity to this claim; they just follow blindly whatever they are told by those they deem to be knowledgeable.

The greenhouse effect occurs in a predominantly closed system because short length infrared, visible and ultraviolet solar radiation enter the greenhouse through the glass or plastic (transparent) windows and are re-emitted as longer wave length infrared radiation that cannot easily escape back through the translucent medium to the outside environment. By preventing the warm air from escaping via convection, a temporary buildup of heat inside the greenhouse occurs. This effect is also very apparent on a sunny day inside a closed car with the windows rolled up. This "greenhouse effect" does not create any new heat during this process; it only holds the heat inside for a longer duration than normal. The Earth's atmosphere is not contained within a closed system but is an open one; consequently, it does not behave as an actual greenhouse. There is a constant movement of the air from areas of high pressure to areas of low pressure. This is mainly caused by the sun's activity, the rotation of the Earth (The Earth is rotating on its axis at approximately 1,000 miles per hour at the equator) and the 23.5° tilt of the Earth's axis.

The Earth's atmosphere (dry) is composed of approximately 78% nitrogen, 21% oxygen and 0.9% argon with all the other gases such as neon, methane, helium and carbon dioxide only accounting for less than 1/10 of 1%. According to these experts, carbon dioxide (presently less than 0.04%) is a major contributor to the warming of the Earth's surface because it reflects the heat from the Sun back to the Earth. They also claim that mankind is the main contributor to any increase, while in reality, the majority of the carbon dioxide in the atmosphere occurs naturally with antropogenic increases of CO_2 contributing an insignificant amount. Water vapor (clouds) in the atmosphere (Approximately 1 to 3% of the atmosphere's total "wet mass") cover about 70% of the entire Earth's surface at any one time and is by far the greatest contributor to this effect. This result becomes clearly apparent by the warming effect produced at night from cloud cover in opposition to the cooling effect on a cloudless night where the heat is allowed to escape unimpeded by the cloud cover. The sun has 333,000 times the mass of the Earth with a volume 1.3 million times that of Earth and is by far the predominant source of all these Earthly phenomenon and the major contributor to all the Earth's climate change.

Air has a molecular weight (g/mol) of 28.97, while carbon dioxide (CO_2) has a molecular weight of 44.01 and hydrogen sulfide gas (H_2S) has a molecular weight of 34.08, both heavier than air. Carbon monoxide (CO) is slightly lighter than air with a molecular weight of 28.01, with the molecular weight of methane (CH_4) at 16.04, helium (He) at 4.02 and hydrogen (H_2) at 2.02, all lighter than air. Gases are free flowing without fixed crystalline structures; they have lower densities than liquids or solids and have no definite shape or volume. Gases do not possess strong nuclear attractions between their atoms like liquids and solids and; therefore, are not attracted to each other. This is why a mixture of different gases, i.e. air, mix uniformly. It would seem that these "scientists" either do not understand the properties of gases or fail to take them into consideration when they proclaim that somehow carbon dioxide forms a blanket in the upper atmosphere that absorbs sunlight and radiates it back to Earth. Even though CO_2 is heavier than air with a density of approximately one and two-thirds that of air, it is long lived and usually well mixed in the atmosphere by diffusion.

Since both carbon dioxide and hydrogen sulfide gases are heavier than air, if they are released near ground level into the atmosphere in large quantities they will tend to settle in low-lying areas first and then slowly disperse into the atmosphere. This is one reason why smokestacks are used to release these gases at a high enough altitude to minimize this tendency. When a leak occurs at a sour gas plant (sour gas contains abundant traces of hydrogen sulfide) the workers are instructed to immediately seek higher ground. This is because the hydrogen sulfide gas will be dispersed at the ground level first and is not prone to immediately mix with the Earth's atmosphere. This is true of carbon dioxide as well. In January 1987, the Los Angeles Times ran an article entitled "1,700 in W. Africa Killed by Poison Gas, Scientists Conclude". The consensus by "scientists" from five countries was that this "poison gas" was odorless, colorless carbon dioxide released from Lake Nios in Cameroon that rapidly swept through the nearby village killing all but four of the residents and at least 300 head of cattle in the region as well. What they failed to mention is that the gas, being heaver than air, hugged the ground and did not immediately disperse into the atmosphere. They mention that the 1,200 villagers, others in nearby areas and cattle died from suffocation which is true since the carbon dioxide displaced all the oxygen and the villagers were asleep during the release, but they did not die from inhaling "poison gas" since carbon dioxide is not a poison regardless of the erroneous position taken by the EPA (Environmental Protection Agency). It is believed that this phenomenon was volcanic in origin and could occur elsewhere, but is not a common occurrence. Eventually heavier than air gases, such as carbon dioxide and hydrogen sulfide, will disperse into the surrounding atmosphere due to winds and the inherent properties of gases.

In reality, the atmosphere is a homogeneous mixture of all the gases. Since there is considerably less than one tenth of one percent of carbon dioxide in the atmosphere to start with, even in their own words these scientists admit that, at most, the carbon dioxide content of the atmosphere has not even come close to approaching a full percent. A doubling of the carbon dioxide content in the atmosphere is still minuscule at best. The total mass of the Earth's atmosphere is about 5.5 quadrillion tons, so a doubling of the amount of carbon dioxide in the atmosphere would require 22 billion tons of carbon dioxide to be added to the atmosphere. This is still a diminutive amount of carbon dioxide (0.0000004%) when compared with the remainder of the atmospheric contents. The actual composition of the atmosphere remains essentially constant with increased altitude, but the total volume of air decreases with an increase in altitude. Since atmospheric pressure decreases with increasing altitude, the air itself becomes less dense (thins out) so there is also subsequently less carbon dioxide present at higher altitudes, not more, as some scientists would have us believe. Due to these factors, there is only a minuscule amount of carbon dioxide at any time in the Earth's upper atmosphere; certainly not enough to cause any noticeable global warming. It is difficult to get these alleged scientists to commit to a consensus as to the altitude at which this imaginary blanket of carbon dioxide forms, but it appears to be at least 17,000 feet above mean sea level and probably considerably higher. Using 17,000 feet as a minimum, the atmospheric density at this altitude is 59% that of sea level density. This means that there are only 59% as many carbon dioxide molecules for every cubic foot of air than at sea level, not more. According to NASA they have instrumentation aboard a satellite that measured an increase of 5 to 12% in the concentration level of carbon dioxide over a ten year period beginning in 2002 in the stratosphere and thermosphere between 50 and 70 miles above the Earth's surface. How is this significant? At these altitudes, there is practically no air and certainly an insignificant amount of carbon dioxide present. If you increase a negligible quantity of carbon dioxide by up to 12%, the end result is still virtually nothing; certainly not enough to cause any noticeable global warming.

Additionally, most of any added carbon dioxide is absorbed by the oceans and plants. Do we really want to decrease the amount of carbon dioxide available to plant life? Plants are the food source for nearly all animals and mankind! A significant reduction in the amount of CO_2 in the air would negatively upset the ecological balance resulting in severe food crop deficiencies. In actuality, there are many factors that contribute to changes in climate, most considerably more influential than the amount of carbon dioxide in the atmosphere. Variables in sun spot activity, water vapor in the atmosphere including cloud coverage, ocean cycles, forestation, natural disasters such as volcanic eruptions and many other factors are much larger contributors to the Earth's climate. Proponents of global warming warn that an increase to 400 ppm (parts per million) of carbon dioxide in the atmosphere will cause a crisis. This claim is not substantiated by history or science. Geological records reveal that during past ice ages levels of carbon dioxide in the atmosphere were at times considerably greater than they are today, as much as 20 times higher. Data obtained from ice core samples in Antarctica indicate that increases in carbon dioxide levels are preceded by global temperature rises. Temperature changes affect the amount of carbon dioxide in the atmosphere, not the other way around. This can be proven scientifically since the saturation level of CO_2 in water (oceans) decreases with a rise in temperature increasing the concentration of CO_2 in the atmosphere. Out gassing of carbon dioxide from oceans is the primary cause of any increase in carbon dioxide levels in the atmosphere, not any minuscule amounts added to the atmosphere as a result of man's activities.

One trouble with much of the so-called scientific data is the manner in which it is obtained. For instance, just recently some scientists took ice bore samples from a small region in the Antarctic. They measured the carbon dioxide levels in entrapped air bubbles that they claim is just as it existed tens of thousands of years ago. From their measurements, they deduced that the carbon dioxide levels from this prehistoric era were considerably lower than they are today. Hence global warming is real! There are a number of reasons why this conclusion bears no semblance to scientific reality. First, how was it determined what ice bore depth corresponds to a particular age? There are numerous factors such as variable yearly precipitation rates and ice compression or melting under different conditions and other parameters that are unknown and could distort the results. No one was there to verify any of this data, so it is suspect from the start. Also, who is to say that a small air sample taken in the Antarctic today is identical to the entire atmosphere that covered the Earth during that time? Is it reasonable to assume that these samples taken over an area of a few square miles at most is characteristic of the entire area of the Earth's surface? A major problem is a self selection sampling bias by these scientists where in many cases only a particular area of concern is being addressed to prove their point. All factors are not taken into consideration to arrive at their desired outcome. One group of scientists will show that the earth is cooling by measuring only mean annual temperatures at specific locations. Another group will only measure polar ocean temperatures and arrive at the conclusion that the earth is warming. By manipulating the data, they can arrive at any conclusion desired and then point to statistical results as their proof. This is not scientific; it is junk science.

Meteorologists cannot even predict local weather accurately a week in advance; in many cases not even a day in advance, yet we are to believe that the climatologists can predict a temperature rise of half a degree Fahrenheit over a 100 year period. Who can predict with certainty that the overall temperature of the Earth will rise continuously for the next hundred years without a reversal? The only scientists that believe this nonsense are those that are using computer generated models based on probability and statistics with the presupposition that mankind will continue to add carbon dioxide to the atmosphere at an unprecedented rate without regard to the many other factors that contribute to climate change. Remember that less than 50 years ago, all these climatologists were warning of an impending ice age, not global warming. How soon we forget!

Carbon dioxide is also being touted as a pollutant by politicians in order to convince people that it is harmful, when in fact it is a naturally occurring beneficial atmospheric trace gas. The EPA (Environmental Protection Agency) has declared carbon dioxide a dangerous pollutant. Does legislation by a corrupt government agency make it a fact? Absolutely not! Humans and animals breathe in air that contains carbon dioxide which is a colorless, odorless trace gas with every breath utilizing the oxygen and exhaling carbon dioxide. If carbon dioxide were in fact a pollutant, all humans and animals would probably have become extinct long ago. Would we be drinking carbonated beverages without impairment if carbon dioxide was a toxin? Do all the animals and the over seven billion humans on Earth pollute the atmosphere too? The EPA monitors six major air pollutants;

ground level ozone, particulate matter, carbon monoxide, lead and oxides of nitrogen and sulfur, as well they should. It is desirable to reduce the level of pollutants in the atmosphere for health reasons, but it is wrong to include carbon dioxide as a pollutant; it is not. Plants utilize carbon dioxide and give off oxygen during photosynthesis, but no new carbon or oxygen is produced. Only the chemical bonds are rearranged to allow the plants to utilize these compounds. Reducing our so called "Carbon Footprint" by reducing the amount of carbon dioxide in the atmosphere does nothing to change the climate significantly; it only reduces the amount available for plant growth. Carbon dioxide is vital to life on Earth.

The problem many people have is in comprehending the vast area of the surface of the Earth in comparison with the areas that are being altered by human intervention. The surface area of the Earth is about 197,000,000 square miles (126 billion acres). Over 70 percent of this is ocean salt water which for all practical purposes is unoccupied by man. Another three percent is covered by fresh water. This leaves just over 57 million square miles of land with the majority, 33 percent being desert and 24 percent mountains. Additionally, forests on the continents as well as the entire continent of Antarctica and most of Australia add considerable areas that are also uninhabited by man. This leaves less than 24,600,000 square miles (15.8 billion acres) of habitable land. Man's influence on the entire surface of the Earth is too small to make a noteworthy difference. The entire seven billion plus population of the world today only covers less than three percent of the total land mass and of that considerably less than one percent produce any major carbon dioxide emissions at any one time. Nature produces about 95% of all carbon dioxide emissions while at most man is only responsible for about 5%, an insignificant amount. The public looks at local neighborhoods, such as large cities, comparatively small areas of deforested land or strip mines, and believe that this human intervention is happening on a massive worldwide scale. This is simply not true! The surface of the Earth is immense. Just to fly over the oceans from one continent to another at a speed of 600 miles per hour takes a considerable number of hours. A few hundred years ago, it couldn't even be done! Now it takes less than ten minutes to fly over the largest cities in the world at this speed. These pseudo-scientists produce fake computer generated maps of major land masses that show most of the land being occupied by man, and being lit up by electric lights at night. That this is not true can be verified by just flying over these areas at night in an airplane. Even in the daytime it is evident that the oceans and the majority of the land masses are not occupied by man or cultivated. The photographs taken at night from the International Space Station (ISS) depict extremely bright lights over large areas of all populated continents. When flying over a major city such as Chicago in an airliner at an altitude of less than 20,000 ft. (1-1/2 percent of the altitude of the ISS) the lights, while unquestionably visible, are not as bright as they would have you believe they are when viewed with the unaided eye from the International Space Station (ISS). What they don't say is how these images were created. The luminosity of the light source from these populated regions is relatively low to begin with and decreases as the inverse square of the distance from the source. Since the average distance of the ISS from the light source is about 248 miles, the light reaching the space station is incredibly weak. Very little light can be seen with the unaided eye at this great a distance from the source because the light diminishes so much due to the inverse square rule. To get the detail they are looking for, they use high magnification cameras to capture small areas over populated regions and then piece together a considerable number of individual frames to arrive at their composite picture which is then edited and enhanced to increase the brightness. Numerous depictions of the Earth's populated areas that are revealed every day by the media on TV illustrate large areas of illumination emanating from the surface with beams radiating out into space like searchlights. Most of the man made light sources such as street lighting, building illumination and vehicle headlights are designed to project light downward or horizontally, not upward. What would be the point if the majority of the lights were pointing skyward? What about time zones? They often portray these lights in a composite photograph with the same intensity on both coasts of the United States as if the Sun's intensity was identical at all locations at the same time when in fact there is a gradient from one longitudinal location to another. Additionally, many of these lights are actually shown to be emanating from areas that are known to be sparsely populated. None of these supposed representations of the Earth's surface as viewed from space ever include cloud cover, which would certainly be visible from the space station located well above the Earth's atmosphere. If these representations were factual, clouds would obscure considerable areas since approximately 67% of the Earth's surface is covered by clouds all of the time.

To get a better understanding as to what can actually be seen from the ISS, one should observe the "Earth Views" broadcast on the NASA television channel. These real time high definition camera views of the Earth's surface are taken from the International Space Station and are telecast many times during each day. These videos, although not actual representations of "naked eye" views, are very close. They are usually views taken out of the front of the ISS, but often are taken looking rearward and occasionally facing downward. Since the ISS is traveling at over 17,000 miles per hour, a lot of ground is covered rapidly;

considerably faster than the Earth's rate of rotation, taking only 90 minutes to transverse a complete orbit of the Earth. Since the Space Station is only 248 miles above the Earth's surface which is only 6% of the Earth's radius (about 4,000 miles), the camera only covers about 3% of the entire Earth's surface at any one time, or just under six million square miles. Although 6,000,000 square miles seems like a lot, it only represents a field of view of about 2,450 miles which is not very large when compared to the visible area of the Earth surface when viewed from afar. Usually what is observed is ocean with considerable cloud cover and the occasional appearance of land masses; often portions of continents. It is nearly impossible to decipher what these land masses are due to all the cloud cover and the small percentage of the land's surface that is visible at any one time from this relatively low altitude. Due to the Earth's apparent brightness in daylight, the aperture of the camera lens must be shuttered down to prevent the picture from being washed out from over exposure. This results in the stars in the sky not being visible since their light is too weak to be captured by the camera with the exposure set to properly view the brighter Earth's surface. This is similar to one not being able to see stars during the daytime on the Earth's surface and is due to the minuscule quantity of light from the stars that reaches the person's eye or the camera's lens. Occasionally views are taken with part of the Earth in darkness and overly bright lights emanating from the surface being shown. This is an example of where the camera captures considerably more light than the human eye and is attributable to over exposure in these areas due to the camera's aperture setting. When views from the ISS are taken facing downward, even less area is observed, but with greater clarity that allows for considerably sharper differentiation between the water and land masses. It is still extremely difficult to determine which land mass is being observed due to all the cloud cover and the small area of land that is under observation. At this distance (248 miles) from the Earth's surface, there is no visible indication of life or man's influence on the Earth's surface in these unmagnified untouched raw images; no visible people, jet aircraft vapor trails, cities, farms, massive structures or ships. Why is it that one can observe aircraft and vapor trails quite easily from Earth, but they are not visible from the ISS without magnification? It is because the aircraft is usually flying at or below 35,000 feet (about 6-1/2 miles) above sea level. The ISS is at an altitude that is over 35 times this far away. If you are not convinced, watch the NASA videos for yourself!

Many people believe, as they are taught by these pseudo-scientists, that the vastly smaller areas of the Earth that are being polluted or damaged by environmental accidents have a significant influence on the health of the planet. This is all utter make-believe nonsense that is intended to deceive the majority of the Earth's populace into believing their deception. In actuality, the Earth has an enormous resiliency and ability to quickly self correct any environmental damage and restore itself. This is evident in how rapidly serious environmental accidents, such as massive oil spills, pollution from factories prior to the introduction of pollution control devices, and toxic releases, as well as natural disasters such as volcanic eruptions, tidal waves, hurricanes, tornadoes, earthquakes and forest fires have dissipated, with little or no help from mankind. Additionally, major wars between countries that last for many years or even decades cause significant localized damage and destruction, but in a relatively short time afterwards the majority of the damage is no longer evident. Great devastation was wrought on the world during major wars, but after less than 80 years, very little, if any, is still recognizable. For instance, the atomic bombing of Hiroshima and Nagasaki and the massive destruction caused during the prolonged Vietnam War is hardly perceptible today. One hundred years is an insignificant amount of time even if compared only to the 6,000 years of recorded history, much less compared to all pre-history. How much environmental damage remains evident from even 100 years ago; how much still from only 1,000 years ago? The world is strong and robust and teeming with life, not small and delicate as numerous misinformed environmentalists would have us believe. Man is not destroying the planet, but only affecting it in inconsequential ways. It will take considerably more effort from man to destroy the planet.

In nearly all instances when the television media shows a video of a coal or nuclear power plant to illustrate to the public how much pollution and carbon dioxide is being dumped into the atmosphere, they picture a row of natural or forced draft cooling towers and not smokestacks. This just goes to show that they either don't know what they are talking about, or have been misled by a politician or someone else with ulterior motives to perpetuate their sham. A large plume is visible exiting the top exhaust of the cooling tower that is produced when the saturated air inside the cooling tower mixes with the cooler ambient air outside. Natural draft cooling towers only emit water vapor, completely devoid of any pollutants or excess carbon dioxide. Due to the significantly large cooling requirements of fossil and nuclear fueled power plants, the cooling towers are the largest manifest structures and the water vapor that is expelled from their tops appears to the uninformed to be pollution, so they exploit this phenomenon to achieve their deception. In developed countries like the United States, coal fired power plant smokestacks are fitted with scrubbers to remove the harmful components and in most cases the final emissions are too small to be considered a major source of pollutants. Consequently they try to fool the public into believing that the cooling towers are a major source of pollution, when in fact they create no pollution what-so-ever. There is no visible pollution coming from the reactors in a nuclear power plant, so they must concentrate on the only visible source of emissions, water vapor from cooling towers, if they are going to try and convince the public of their deception. In under developed countries and some developing countries, such as large highly populated cities in India and China, the smokestacks from coal fired power plants are a major local source of pollution and a real health concern and should be fitted with scrubbers to remove the bulk of the pollutants, but it is not necessary or even desirable to spend money for the removal of carbon dioxide which is not a pollutant and not a significant contributor to global warming.

The pseudo-scientists like to show how the sea levels are rising due to global warming and how they will eventually cause all our shores to be flooded under hundreds of feet of water. There is; however, no evidence that this is happening. They claim that glaciers are retreating, permafrost is melting, and sea ice is disappearing. Yes, many of the arctic glaciers are receding, but that is only a small part of the overall picture and does not produce any significant increases in the water level of entire oceans. While the western Arctic appears to be getting somewhat warmer, Greenland and parts of the eastern Arctic are actually getting colder. In late 2016, scientists claimed that the percentage of ice covering the Arctic Ocean in that year that melted during the warmer months tied the record for the greatest decrease in coverage since 2007. What they fail to express, in hopes that it will be missed, is that this indicates that for all the years between 2007 and 2016 (a total of 8 years) and all the years prior to 2007, the percentage of ice covering the Arctic Ocean that melted in these years was obviously less. This doesn't bode well for their premise that the quantity of ice covering the Arctic Ocean is continuing to decrease every year due to climate change. They like to point out how large chunks of the leading edge of glaciers are constantly breaking off. This is a normal daily phenomenon that is known as "calving", not something new. Localized melting of permafrost and sea ice occurs on a yearly basis, due to variations in the annual climate. This is normal and does not signify a major and lasting overall warming effect. Also, periodic fluctuations such as El Nino do not characterize climate change.

Quite a few years ago these pseudo-scientists were claiming that there would be a considerable increase in the number and intensity of hurricanes due to climate changes caused by man's burning of fossil fuels and other potential Earth warming activities. If an increase in hurricane activity is caused by man, why did Florida experienced its first mild hurricane at the beginning of September 2016 after a hiatus of 11 years? Yes, the third worst hurricane in U.S. history was Katrina that occurred in 2005, but it was only a category 3. It caused so much devastation because it hit New Orleans, Louisiana and caused record storm surge up to 28 feet. The damage was widespread not because of its wind strength, but because the city of New Orleans is below sea level and the levee and flood walls that protect the municipality were breached allowing the storm surge to devastate the city. The hurricane that claimed the greatest loss of life at up to 12,000 deaths was the Galveston, Texas category 4 hurricane of 1900. The hurricane with the highest wind speed to hit the U.S. was Camille in 1969 with wind speeds estimated at 190 mph at landfall. So, the majority of hurricanes with the greatest wind speeds, rainfall associated with flooding and storm surge are not taking place more frequently, but occurred considerably earlier. It doesn't appear that they got this theory right either! Although there is no tangible evidence to substantiate it, some scientists say that sea levels have risen up to eight inches over the past hundred years. Eight inches in 100 years is not very much. If a low land area or island is periodically being flooded by this small of an increase, then that land must be only slightly above sea level to begin with. It should not have been inhabited in the first place since it has always been well below the flood plain level. In numerous cases such as the Marshall Islands, Republic of Maldives and Tuvalu, these low land areas consist of strips of land no more than a few hundred feet in width. For instance, Tuvalu consists of coral reef islands and atolls with a total land area of only 10 square miles. The highest point is 15 feet above sea level with an average elevation of 6 feet. To get some perspective, the land area of Manhattan Island is nearly 23 square miles with an average elevation of 62 feet above sea level. In some instances, such as the Seychelles Islands, the sea level is not rising substantially, but the islands are actually sinking. This is not a result of climate change. Most of the receding of our beaches is caused by erosion from wind and high water levels during storm surge from hurricanes and tsunamis, not from global warming or permanent rising ocean levels. This talk about rising sea levels is the result of falsification of data from incorrect computer modeling, not from actual observations or measurements. They also say that they have measured that the overall temperature of the Earth has increased by just under 1° Celsius since 1880 and that it is continuing to increase at an alarming rate. There is no indication that this is happening either. They show how they have measured these temperature rises all around the world and would like the public to believe that they can make accurate temperature measurements within less than 1° Celsius. They can; their instruments are extremely accurate, but their data acquisition methods are not. Even the daily random passage of clouds over a site will change the temperature reading in excess of this amount and distort the accuracy of their readings. Any alteration in the surrounding environment, such as the addition of nearby buildings or roads, the change in the adjacent plant coverage, or the amount of rain or snow fall occurring over a short time span can change the outcome more than the fractional temperature changes recorded, rendering the data useless. These scientists state that they have ascertained that this overall temperature rise of 1° Celsius began with the industrial age from temperature readings made over centuries. What they fail to say is where these temperatures were recorded. For their readings to be significant, they would have to be recorded at the exact same location for literally hundreds of years without any meaningful changes to the surrounding topography or environment. This is not possible. The population of the world has increased exponentially in the past 150 years and conditions where these measurements were originally made have changed drastically. One hundred and fifty years ago, there were no paved roads, no automobiles, no aircraft and very little power consumption compared with today. Most of the population was agrarian and the cities that did exist were much smaller. Many of their readings are taken at airports today that didn't even exist when they claim these readings were first being documented. Also, their instrumentation was nowhere near as accurate then as it is today. If you look at the daily TV weather channel, you will notice that considerably more often than not, the record high temperature for that day occurs at an earlier date than the record low temperature. Quite often the highest recorded temperature on any given day was more than 50 to 100 years ago with the lowest temperature on record occurring more recently or within a few years of the highest recorded temperature for that day. More recently there have been a number of days with new record high temperatures recorded. Quite often, these new highs replaced previous maximum temperatures that occurred a considerable number of years ago. New higher highs are not being recorded recently year after year as they would have you believe.

Additionally, recent record new low temperatures are being recorded just as often as the new highs. They either don't report this, or they try to explain that these too are somehow caused by excessive warming of the planet. This is not an indication of massive global warming. The major contributor to climate change on Earth is caused by our Sun and other natural factors, not by a minuscule increase in carbon dioxide levels whether caused by man or any other means. Recently, it was revealed, that in actuality, the average worldwide temperature has been decreasing every year since 1999, not increasing. Also, that the ice coverage in the Arctic and Antarctica is increasing, not decreasing, but they choose to ignore these facts since they already have their minds made up that global warming is a real and present danger. The politicians have done a good job in brain washing the public since now they have convinced most of the nation's leaders and the United Nations as well that global warming is a serious threat created by man. Nothing concerning climate change could be further from the truth. The current hysteria related to global warming by man's intervention is unfounded and most likely contrived. The general public has seem to forgotten that as short a time as 40 years ago these renowned scientists were all predicting a coming ice age, not global warming. Global climates are continually changing. This is a normal phenomenon; it is a natural occurrence that is not being significantly altered by man except in small isolated instances.

Another supporter of climate change with an opposing view is the author of the book Dark Winter, John L. Casey. He takes a contradictory outlook from the global warming extremists with the view that ominous changes will take place soon due to decreased sunspot activity. His assumption is based on a statistical analysis of past solar activity cycles and consists primarily of a "solar hibernation" or "grand minimum" caused by a substantial reduction of the Sun's activity or output with a cold period lasting between 22 to 33 years and repeating about every 206 years. Casey makes predictions of colder climates up to 100,000 years or more into the future without any credible scientific backup. In 2007 he theorized that another solar minimum will start in the next 3 to 14 years, predicting that it should have begun by 2010 or 2011, but there is no substantial evidence of this happening even as late as 2017. According to Casey in 2007 NASA and NOAA made satellite measurements of a new record abrupt temperature drop in ocean temperatures that supports his forecast for a record global temperature reduction by December 2012. Casey states that " ...the end of the current 206-year cycle should be obvious to all by 2012." It hasn't happened; at least not yet! His RC (Relational Cycles) theory is supposedly based on available data on the Sun's behavior and how we can measure it going back 1,200 years. As stated by Casey himself in his book, "There is no proof of RC theory without relying on carbon dating, no 206-year cycle and no ability to predict the solar hibernation of the 21st century". His entire theory depends on the premise that carbon dating provides an accurate method for determining age which in reality has been shown to be unreliable. Casey suggests that science on climate change is being classified as either politically correct or not these days instead of relying on sound professional research; this is obviously true. He asserts that Antarctica has been getting much colder and has been doing so for a long time with seasionally average surface air temperature decreasing by 0.7 degrees Celsius per decade. This is incompatable with Al Gore's 2008 claim that the entire North Polar ice cap will be gone in 5 years. In his book he displays a chart of the last 200 year sunspot activities overlaid with a formula derived curve for the 206-year bicentennial cycle. This chart is misleading since the highest sunspot activities for the formula derived curve are shown occurring at areas of actual recorded lower sunspot activity with total disregard for these anomalies. Casey asserts that there is not only the 206-year solar hibernation cycle, but also smaller cycles of 90 to 100 years, 60, 20 and 9 years as well that influence Earth's climate. These cycles are supposedly related to the motion of the planets around the Sun as well as the Moon around the Earth. In early 2008, several institutions that monitor global temperatures specified that they measured drops in global temperatures for the previous year of approximately 0.5° Celsius. Their temperature drop estimates varied between 0.588 and 0.643 degrees. What is significant about these figures is not only the considerable range of temperature measurements by different agencies of over 9%, but the publication of their results to three decimal places. There is no possible way their results could be accurate to three decimal places and vary by over 9% between the various agencies. This is just another example of inaccurate data, and a misunderstanding of significant figures in computations resulting in values representing more precision than can be justified.

Although the media reports the melting of the glaciers in Greenland on a regular basis, Casey argues that what they don't say is that, in fact, the ice sheets in the interior of Greenland are growing and have been doing so since around 1992. Environmentalists and other uninformed alarmists are proclaiming that the polar bear population is dwindling and will soon become extinct owing to loss of habitat due to the melting of Arctic sea ice. According to Casey, what they don't say is that the truth is that in the mid 1960s, the polar bear population was estimated to be about 10,000 whereas for more than the last 40 years the polar bear population has remained stable between 20,000 and 25,000. According to Casey, the northern lights (Aurora Borealis) can be used as an indicator of the Sun's output and has declined to a 100 year low. Recently; however, this phenomenon has been observed as far south as the northern regions of the continental United States. Again, just as in the euphoria created by global warming advocates, he doesn't take into account all the factors involved in climate change. Similar to his contemporaries, he takes a narrow view of one factor involving climate change, in this case sunspot activity, and ignores or gives little credence to the rest. This approach is doomed to failure and is not scientific; just as with the global warming advocates, all factors must be considered and taken into account to arrive at a sound conclusion. NASA and NOAA regularly revise their estimates of sunspot activity to more closely agree with actual events and readily admit that the root cause and energy transfer mechanisms within the Sun are not well understood. In addition to long range seasonal changes, there are daytime and nocturnal changes where the heat energy from the Sun varies during the day due to cloud cover and local conditions including whether the underlying surface is water or land and what type of topography is being impacted. Winter is occurring in the southern hemisphere during the same time that the northern hemisphere is experience summer; temperatures worldwide are always increasing in some areas and decreasing in others. Climate is changing all the time; that is a fact and it is a normal occurrence. What is fiction is that it is being changed for the worst by man's contribution. During some years there is greater wind activity in the form of more powerful hurricanes, tornadoes, typhoons, or other wind storms than previous years. They do not; however, become stronger each and every year, nor do they occur with greater frequency every year. This is also true of all other phenomenon associated with climatic conditions such as dust storms, forest fires, glacial melting and higher daily temperatures.

Bill Nye, also known as the "Science Guy" is another adamant believer that anthropogenic global warming is real and an imminent threat to all mankind. He has a BSME degree and a mechanical engineering background and is highly regarded by some as a scientific educator since he has taught basic science to grade school students on TV which only requires a rudimentary knowledge of basic physics, but not climatology. He expresses highly opinionated views on evolution, the Big Bang theory and global climate change without going into details as to why he holds such an adamant opinion on his beliefs or offering any scientific backup. He is so resolute in his beliefs on global warming that he advocates that those with opposing views are "Climate Change Deniers". This of course is sheer nonsense since viturally everyone is quite aware that climate change is real, just not a result of mankind's inappropriate use of resources or that it is necessarily environmentally detrimental. He believes that anyone who disagrees with him should not only be censored and not allowed to express an opposing viewpoint, but that they should be incarcerated! This is ludicrous and does not embrace the scientific method; it is just another example of retaliation against individuals with opposing views.

There are two diametrically opposed theories for climate change; that of AGW (Anthropogenic Global Warming) that says that man is responsible for global warming at an unprecedented rate and Casey's RC (Relational Cycles) hypothesis that relates to global cooling. So called "experts" blame man-made global warming for record snowfalls coupled with record cold temperatures. Casey essentially says the opposite, indicating that record high temperatures precede record lows. Regardless of their viewpoint, they want it both ways! Both Al Gore and John Casey are declaring a planetary crisis that requires immediate action but, for the opposite reasons. Who is right; very probably neither? For over the past hundred years, our climate changes have been very mild; prior to that time the changes were more pronounced. It is more likely that we are just returning to more normal climate patterns.

More recently, In 2017, a geologist by the name of Gregory Wrightstone published a book entitled "Inconvenient Facts" which outlines 60 reasons why anthropogenic global warming, (the part contributed to mankind's burning of fossil fuels and other releases of CO_2 into the Earth's atmosphere) is not valid as a contributor to global warming. He also shows, with the help of numerous graphs and illustrations, why CO_2 is not causing runaway global warming and that increased CO_2 levels are not only not dangerous, but advantageous to man and our planet. His book mainly provides a history of CO_2 levels and their relationship to temperatures in the past along with current trends and their implications. One concern is that some of his graphs and conclusions are based on information obtained from Antarctic ice core samples that are suspect since there is no creditable information or conclusions that can be ascertained from periods billions or even millions of years in the past. Any conclusions from considerably earlier than prerecorded history that are reached based from data collected in our current geological period are purely conjecture or unproven theories. Fortunately; however, he includes a considerable number of graphs that contain published information from more recent periods that provide a convincing argument for his assertions.

He provides data that implies that the level of CO_2 in the atmosphere for our current Quaternary geological period is too low and is actually approaching the minimum survival threshold for vegetation where most terrestrial plant life cannot exist providing a convincing argument for the benefit of increased carbon dioxide levels, not lower. He shows that during the medieval warm periods and little ice age that occurred between

1000 AD and 1900 AD global CO_2 levels were lower than today and did not demonstrate any direct correlation between CO_2 quantities in the atmosphere and global temperature levels. His graphs and charts indicate that global warming began over 250 years before the Industrial Revolution, meaning that our current temperature increases are not unusual, unprecedented, or man-made.

He demonstrates why the melting of glaciers that form icebergs in the Arctic Ocean will not result in a significant increase in worldwide sea levels. This is because when water freezes and becomes ice, it transforms to an ordered regular crystalline structure that is less dense than the water it displaces resulting in an approximately 9% increase in volume over an equal mass of water. Additionally, there is usually entrapped air in the ice further increasing the volume of water displaced. About nine-tenths of an iceberg is submerged in the water with only about 10 to 15% above the surface (depending upon the salinity of the water). When the ice below the surface of the water melts, the volume of the water remaining is about 9% less and the added volume of the ice that was originally above the surface adds an additional 9 to 10% resulting in an overall net gain in water level that is insignificant. This is true in the Arctic, because this is ocean ice, not located on land. The Antarctic ice is primarily on land (the Antarctic continent) which is the fifth largest continent on Earth (Europe and Australia are smaller). The Arctic is an ocean surrounded by continents, while Antarctica is a continent surrounded by water. Although the Antarctic is a desert and receives very little annual snowfall, if the ice sheets on the Antarctic continent which are thousands of feet thick melted, it would contribute to a rise in ocean levels. However, the ice levels on the Antarctic continent are not decreasing but increasing and the average temperature in the Antarctic is about 30° Celsius lower than the Arctic.

His book is recommended reading to acquire an inclusive historic viewpoint on why climate change is not an issue that requires immediate drastic action as some claim, but rather why anthropogenic global warming is a manufactured deception.

One of the latest irresponsible proposals by some members of Congress to combat "global warming" is to eliminate all cows and bulls worldwide since they contend that methane traps heat and that the amount of methane released into the atmosphere through their flatulence is so great as to impose a genuine threat to significant warming of the Earth's surface. Actually, they emit mostly methane during burping (95%) and only 5% from flatulence. According to their theory, the 1.5 billion cows worldwide each emit between 70 and 120 kilograms per year of methane. Since methane is a trace gas and only accounts for 0.00018% (1,800 parts/billion) of the total Earth's atmosphere, it amounts to considerably less than the total percentage of CO_2 (under 0.04%) in the atmosphere. The amount of methane in the atmosphere, even if twice the amount present 150 years ago, is still minuscule. Neither CH_4 nor CO_2 occur in sufficient quantities to produce anthropogenic global warming. Water vapor in clouds is opaque and blocks incoming light from the Sun during the daytime and restricts the release of heat during nighttime hours. Both CH_4 and CO_2 are gasses that are invisible to the human eye and that only occur in minute amounts, so how do they block solar radiation? Some scientists claim that methane is only undetectable by the human eye in the visible spectrum of light, but is opaque to thermal radiation in the ultraviolet spectrum; however, no one has offered a reasonable explanation as to how methane traps heat; just that it does. Maybe laboratory or computer programs can offer theories that seem plausible, but not observations under real atmospheric conditions. Scientific concepts must be based on experience and evidence, not by reason or on theory alone. They claim that methane (CH_4) is 23 times more harmful than carbon dioxide (CO_2), but also state that methane mixes with oxygen and is gradually transformed nearly completely into CO_2 and water vapor (H_2O) over a period of about 9 years. What they fail to mention is that when the CH_4 is converted to CO_2, doesn't that mean that after conversion it becomes considerably less harmful? Additionally, their guesstimates as to how much methane is in the atmosphere as the result of human intervention and its harmfulness in relation to carbon dioxide are all over the place with no definitive consensus. The population of the United States amount to only about 5% of the World's population, so even if we eliminated all cows and bulls in the U.S. it wouldn't make a considerable difference in reducing total bovine emissions. Does anyone really think that the rest of the World would give up all their livestock for this preposterous attempt to reduce perceived global warming? What is the probability that even a minority of U.S. residents would give up hamburgers, steak, barbecue, milk, ice cream, cheese, butter, yogurt, leather, or countless other dairy products? Does anyone in Congress have any idea what they are talking about or realize the impact this would have on the U.S. economy? Obviously not! Many scientists are in agreement that in the U.S. anthropogenic sources of methane emissions are stabilizing. They also say that worldwide levels seem to be leveling off as well. Some contribute this to the fall of the Soviet Union. What nonsense! So if worldwide levels of methane are stabilizing, why is this a problem that requires such drastic action?

In summary, what are some of the major facts that challenge the alleged "Green House" deception that global warming is real and is caused by man's increased burning of fossil fuels? 1) The claim that global warming has been scientifically established and is primarily caused by mankind cannot be backed up with verifiable facts. 2) The Earth's atmosphere behaves as an open system, not as an actual greenhouse which is a closed system. 3) Carbon dioxide makes up less than 0.04% of the Earth's atmosphere and at most a minute amount may be attributable to mankind's intervention. 4) Even though carbon dioxide is heavier than air, it does not have a tendency to form layers in the upper atmosphere, but forms a homogeneous mixture with the atmosphere 5) There are many factors such as sun spot activity, atmospheric water vapor including cloud coverage, ocean cycles, forestation and natural disasters such as massive forest fires and volcanic eruptions that are considerably greater contributors to the Earth's climate than man's intervention. 6) Data and air samples are often taken on a self selection basis to prove a predisposed assertion without regard for fact. 7) Carbon dioxide has been declared a dangerous pollutant by the EPA when in fact it is a beneficial trace gas and not a toxin. 8) Due to the immense surface of the Earth, mankind's influence is far too small to generate any significant carbon dioxide emissions even if it were a valid concern. 9) The Earth has an enormous resiliency with the ability to quickly transform any environmental damage and restore itself. 10) Temperature changes affect the amount of carbon dioxide in the atmosphere, not the other way around. 11) Far too little carbon dioxide exists at higher altitudes to be of any significance in promoting climate change due to the extreme thinning of the entire atmosphere with increased elevation above the Earth's surface. 12) History does not provide convincing evidence to collaborate global warming, either anthropogenic or otherwise.

Another concern by "scientists" that occurred prior to the recent climate change anxiety was the ozone layer depletion supposedly caused by man's irresponsible release of CFC's into the atmosphere.

The stratospheric ozone layer serves as a shield that protects humans and the ecosystem from harmful ultraviolet B (UVB) radiation emitted by the Sun. This ozone layer consists of molecules of O_3 that absorbs ultraviolet light energy from the Sun and turns it into heat. This is why the stratosphere is stratified and gets hotter with an increase in altitude. Atmospheric temperatures range from about - 60° Fahrenheit at lower elevations (4 miles above sea level at the poles to 12 miles at the Equator) to - 5° Fahrenheit at its upper extremities (about 31 miles above sea level). At the elevation of the stratosphere, only about 19% of the atmosphere is present and the concentration of ozone only occurs in small amounts of a few hundred parts per trillion.

There is a falsehood being perpetuated by many scientists that there is a hole in the ozone layer over Antarctica that has been caused by man's irresponsible use of chlorofluorocarbons (CFCs) that are nontoxic atoms containing chlorine, fluorine and carbon. This fabrication states that the ozone hole was caused by the negligent release of CFCs from aerosol spray cans, solvents, refrigerators and air conditioning units into the atmosphere. Apparently, these minute amounts of extremely volatile chemicals somehow migrated down to the Antarctic from more populated areas of the world and destroyed a large area of the ozone layer. There are a number of things wrong with this theory. According to the theory, CFCs are so inert that there is nothing in the troposphere that can capture or destroy them, so consequently they are very long lived. The theory further states that eventually the CFCs are broken down into free chlorine atoms by ultraviolet rays. These chlorine atoms then break down the ozone molecules in a catalytic reaction where according to the U.S. Environmental Protection Agency, hundreds of thousands of ozone molecules are destroyed by each solitary chlorine molecule. This is all conjecture and has never been observed in the laboratory or nature. This theory never predicted nor can it explain the existence of an ozone hole over the Antarctic. This theory consists only of compilations of chemical and mathematical processes that profess to represent the behavior of the atmosphere and its workings, not those observed in the real world. Actually, the ozone layer has never had a hole in it, just a thinning of a small layer over the South Pole in Antarctica that these scientists refer to as a hole.

Moreover, it is claimed that this "Ozone Hole" is responsible for many additional cases of melanoma skin cancer due to a greater amount of the sun's harmful radiation being able to penetrate the Earth's atmosphere. Where is the logical explanation for this statement? The greatest number of people exposed to the Sun's radiation live in the warmer locations on Earth considerably removed from the "Ozone Hole". Very few people live anywhere in Antarctica for any length of time and there are no permanent residents. Antarctica has never had an indigenous population. There are only a few people that spend any time in Antarctica; tourists and those that work at scientific research stations. There are no towns, cities or business enterprises. Those that go there are not inclined to sunbathe and are covered from head to toe with heavy clothing most of the time when outdoors. When working outside at the South Pole, it is essential to protect the skin from frostbite at all times, not sunburn or ultra-violet (UV) radiation from the Sun. The majority of people that get melanoma skin cancer don't live in the Sun Belt or the tropics, but in cooler, more temperate regions of the remaining six continents on Earth that do not receive as much sunlight. This is most likely due to a lack of adequate vitamin D levels caused by less exposure to the sun's rays, not more.

There are a number of axioms and hypotheses that are required to prove the ozone depletion theory. If any of these are confirmed incorrect the entire theory becomes suspect. Some of these incorrect assumptions state that enhanced UV radiation is responsible for an increase in malignant melanoma skin cancer, that the ozone layer is not influenced by solar events or atmospheric energy including electrochemical reactions in the stratosphere, and that there are no natural sources of chlorine or sinks for CFCs other than in the stratosphere. This is not true, and those that embrace this theory dismiss these facts or choose to minimize their importance by stating that they are insignificant. This is a clear example of where mathematical system analysis performed by computer models is used to replace scientific theory. Whatever appears on the computer monitor is taken to be reality without regard for any real world observations or established scientific truths.

Today, considerably more is understood concerning the Antarctic "Ozone Hole" that was previously known. It is now recognized as a naturally occurring seasonal phenomenon that forms in the spring when the atmosphere heats up and reactions between ozone and ozone-depleting substances increase. The thickness of the ozone layer increases again during the winter months. Since the discovery of the seasonal ozone thinning in the Antarctic, additional holes have been revealed occurring over the Arctic and Tibet. The Antarctic "Ozone Hole" is actually shrinkin and is expected to disappear around the year 2040. Regardless of the scientific advancements made there still remains the fact that at least 60% of all observed ozone depletion is due to an unknown mechanism, not man's irresponsible release of CFCs.

7

FOSSIL FUELS VERSUS RENEWABLE ENERGY SOURCES

F ossil fuels are considered to be non-renewable sources of energy. Even though they are continually being replaced through natural processes, the process is so slow as to require considerably more time to restore than the rate that they are being depleted. Recently, more fossil fuel resources have been discovered and more economical and resourceful ways of extracting them have been developed. For this reason, fuels such as coal, oil and natural gas are currently considerably cheaper and more viable methods of supplying our energy needs than alternate methods.

Alternate energy sources such as wind, solar and hydro-electric power generation, although renewable sources of energy, have a considerable number of inherent problems that render them impractical on a large scale. One of these hurdles that needs to be overcome to make alternate energy sources viable is initial cost. Since a windmill is an intermittent source of energy, you cannot make a direct cost comparison with a steady power source such as coal or natural gas. The expenditure to construct a single giant windmill is considerable, especially when the high cost of construction and meager gains obtained are taken into consideration. A windmill only works when the wind is blowing with an adequate force to generate electricity; wind cannot dispatch energy in response to demand. If the wind is too strong, that is a problem too and the windmill must temporarily be taken out of service to prevent damage. During the time when the wind is insufficient or too high and the unit is out of service, no energy is produced so the energy must be stored to provide adequate electricity around the clock. This requires further expenditures and complicates the retrieval and distribution of the energy produced to obtain power grid reliability. For a windmill to provide a viable source of energy, it must be located in an area that receives a reliable year round supply of wind that is relatively constant. A single windmill does not produce enough energy. To even replace a small fossil fueled power plant, a windmill farm consisting of hundreds of giant windmills would be required. A considerable outlay of materials, construction, installation and infrastructure that is extremely costly is required just for one windmill farm. To try to replace a significant percentage of fossil fueled power plants with windmill farms is unrealistic. Additionally, where does the energy required to run the factories that produce the tens of thousands of windmills required come from? Where will all the materials, including the rare earth elements required come from? All these things take energy that must be supplied by fossil fueled plants until an adequate renewable energy source is established. Windmill farms currently supply only a small percentage of mankind's worldwide energy requirements and currently are unfeasible as a comprehensive replacement for conventional power plants. In addition, due to the high cost to produce windmills and their meager output in comparison with conventional fossil fueled power sources, the only way to compete in the power generation grid is if the energy from the windmill farms is heavily subsidized by the government creating an unnecessary financial burden on the taxpayers and/ or customers. The overall cost of a wind turbine including the original cost of the massive tower structure, rotor blades and electrical generating equipment along with the ancillary storage facilities and subsidized pricing is significantly higher than the cost of electricity that can be obtained from conventional coal, natural gas or hydroelectric power plants.

Solar power, whether obtained from solar cells or mirror farms that concentrate the Sun's rays to a single focal point to power steam generators, is also not a viable solution for replacing fossil fuels with a renewable energy source. Solar panels are not only very expensive to produce for the quantity of electrical energy obtained, but they are very inefficient, deteriorate rapidly and only work when there is an adequate source of sunshine. Solar cells don't operate at night and are dramatically less efficient when the sky is overcast. It would literally take millions of them to replace a single conventional fossil fuel power plant along with all the necessary associated ancillary equipment required to store the electricity during periods of downtime plus energy conversion and distribution facilities. They are also impractical as a large scale energy source in a considerable portion of the World's land areas due to the negative effects of extreme latitude on available hours of operation. At the equator, the number of daylight hours is about equal to the number of nocturnal hours year round. As latitudes increase to the north or south of the equator, the number of hours of sunlight in the summer increases the farther away from the equator you go. However, in the winter months, the opposite is true. Adverse weather conditions also have an undesirable effect on power output. The drain on natural resources and rare earth materials to construct the number of solar cells required to replace many of the fossil fuel power plants presently supplying our energy needs today would be staggering, if even possible. Solar panels presently provide an energy source that is useful for areas that are off the grid from major power plants and as a means of charging batteries when electricity is not available from more reliable sources. Mirror farms are also impractical as a major energy source. Not only are they also affected by adverse weather and the lack of sunlight at night, but a massive expenditure outlay is necessary to manufacture them and a large land footprint is required for their mirror farm. They must be located in areas that receive considerable sunlight year-round, such as those found in desert regions, devoid of extended periods of unfavorable climatic conditions.

Windmills, solar panels and mirror farms have considerably lower energy densities than conventional fossil fuels making them ineffective as replacements for sizable energy sources such as power plants and rendering them unsuitable as substitutes due to cost restraints.

An excellent source of renewable energy is hydro-electric power generation. This method of obtaining electricity is advantageous in some locations, but it too has some major drawbacks. There are a limited number of sites available that meet the necessary requirements for the successful construction of a hydro-electric plant. First, an adequate source of water is necessary. In most instances a suitable dam must then be constructed and all of the ancillary equipment including the turbine generators and power transmission lines must be provided at a considerable cost outlay. To attempt to supply even a small percentage of the necessary energy network for even a small country is not only impractical, but entirely unattainable due to the limited locations available, the considerable cost involved and the enormity of natural resources consumed in the construction.

Nuclear power plants are a viable source of power generation. They require fuel, but only small quantities. There are definite drawbacks to producing energy utilizing nuclear fission. The fuel source is limited and difficult to obtain. Spent fuel is highly radioactive and must be disposed of in a safe and responsible manner. Nuclear power plants are very expensive and time consuming to construct and numerous safeguards are required to prevent melt down or release of radioactive material into the atmosphere. If constructed properly, nuclear power plants provide a clean alternative to fossil fuel based power generation, but replacing the entire power grid of all or even most nations is unrealistic, if not impossible.

Geothermal power generation from underground thermal sources provides good clean, renewable alternate energy since it harnesses power from the Earth itself. Heat from the Earth's core averages over 6,000 degrees Fahrenheit and can be accessed up to three miles below the Earth's surface, where it is brought up as steam and used to turn electrical generating turbines. These geothermal power generation facilities are located mainly in Iceland, Indonesia, Italy, Mexico, the Philippines and the United States. Although this is one of the oldest and widely used renewable energy sources, the supply of underground steam is only readily accessible in limited regions of the world making it impractical as a viable replacement for all, or even small-scale hydrocarbon based energy production in most locations world-wide.

Some uninformed critics of oil, gas and other hydrocarbon products would prefer to eliminate them entirely "to save the planet" if they had their way. What they don't seem to understand is that even if all our power requirements could be met by alternate sources, which they cannot, the world would still require large amounts of these conventional hydrocarbon products. They are used in the production of automotive, aviation and other motor and machinery lubricants, tires, tar, asphalt, paraffin wax, isopropyl alcohol, paints, solvents and paint thinners, medicines, shampoos, perfumes, and plastics to name just a few as well as many other non-energy related products. Propane, butane and natural gas must still be used in more remote areas beyond the electric grid to provide a reliable energy source in addition to supplying heating requirements when the Sun is obscured by clouds or inclement weather. Hydrocarbons are used for emergency backup power for when the primary power grid is down. Is it practical to fly airliners strictly with electricity as their only power source? No; and even if it were possible, do we want to go back to propeller driven aircraft utilizing heavy battery packs? So far, no one has been able to come up with a practical way to power a reaction engine that generates thrust by jet propulsion solely on electricity. It would be extremely difficult to wage war with only electric powered vehicles such as tanks and troop carriers as well as ships and aircraft. Maybe this is a good thing! Where will the electricity come from to recharge all the batteries on these conveyances in the battlefield, on the sea or in the air during conflict? How long will it take to charge these batteries with today's present technology? Furthermore, we do not have the technology to fabricate space vehicles that can operate exclusively on electric power. None of these feats are plausible with our present technology and are unlikely to be so for the foreseeable future.

Some automobiles now operate with electric power as their only means of propulsion, but it is unlikely that they will ever become practical for long range use unless some major obstacles are overcome. The most obvious short comings are where to recharge the batteries in remote locations far from metropolitan areas and the length of time required to recharge the batteries. If a gasoline or diesel powered method of conveyance runs out of fuel in a rural area it is a simple matter to bring enough fuel to the vehicle to resume its journey, or to even carry spare fuel.

If an electric automobile runs out of fuel in a remote location, it is not practical to bring an adequate amount of electricity to the remote location and it is presently impractical to carry ample spare batteries. You could bring an electric generator, but it would in all likelihood be powered by a gasoline or diesel powered energy source and would require an unacceptable period of time to sufficiently recharge the vehicle's batteries. Presently, transportation exclusively powered by electricity may be realistic in some urban areas, but not in the countryside. This may change in the future, but it will take a substantial increase in support infrastructure to make this practicable. Another concern is that the batteries that power these electric motors lose a considerable amount of their capacity in extremely cold weather. Many environmentalists that believe that electric vehicles are totally non-polluting are just not using common sense. Where do they think all this electricity comes from? Yes, electric automobiles can to some extent help clean up automotive pollution in inner-cities, but this just requires larger rural power plants to handle the greater electrical grid requirements of the city. Electric cars are only as practical as their source of electricity. If a fossil fueled power plant needs to be doubled in size to handle the additional electric powered cars on the road, these electric cars are not as efficient as proposed by the proponents of electric cars being non-polluting. They are only relocating the small multiple sources of pollution from each automobile to one single dense source at a different more remote location. Presently, gasoline and diesel powered vehicle emissions have been cleaned up by nearly 99% from levels prior to the pollution control era beginning in 1970. What practical gains are to be made by reducing this final 1%? Even if this remaining 1% could be reduced by half, the total reduction in the emissions would only amount to 0.5% of the total. This is not a cost effective or realistic goal.

The Sun is a source of an immense amount of renewable energy, greater than all renewable and nonrenewable sources available on Earth combined. In all likelihood someday more realistic methods of extracting this energy will become feasible. Unfortunately it just isn't practical today with our limited scientific and technological knowledge in this area. For now, the most feasible method of providing the plethora of energy required worldwide are power plants that use current technology utilizing nonrenewable energy sources with scrubbers on coal fired power plant smoke stacks and suitable pollution control on gas and oil fired power plants. Hydroelectric and nuclear power plants can also provide clean energy at low cost once constructed. Hydroelectric power is limited in scope due to the lack of suitable sites available. Nuclear power plants muster considerable opposition from many people due to the potential consequences when a failure does occur. It is; therefore, prudent to continue to use the available nonrenewable energy resources such as coal, oil and gas until such a time as renewable energy sources become more feasible in adequate quantities. There are presently enough nonrenewable energy sources to last another 100 to 200 years at our present rate of consumption. Hopefully, before these nonrenewable energy sources are exhausted, mankind will have solved the problem of efficiently extracting abundant energy from the Sun in the quantities required and be able to store it efficiently. Our present capacitor technology is not adequate to replace batteries as a suitable means of long term electrical storage. They have extremely high self discharge rates, are very expensive, have low energy density compared to lead acid or lithium batteries and they are not capable of utilizing all the energy stored in them. Batteries are not a good source of stored energy either even though to date it is our best method. With all our innovative technological advancements in storage battery development, they are currently too heavy, incorporate high initial cost coupled with relatively short life spans, have unacceptable usable range before discharge and excessive charge times that makes them impractical except in limited applications. There are research facilities presently investigating devices that integrate the energy density of batteries with the added characteristics of high power capacitors. In the future this may lead to energy storage devices that are not only smaller and lighter than existing ones, but may combine the advantages of present day batteries and capacitors; however, this work is presently in its infancy.

8

WHY THE EARTH IS UNIQUE AMONG ALL PLANETS WITHIN THE COSMOS

The planet Earth is unique among not only all the planets contained within our Solar System or even the known regions of our own Milky Way Galaxy, but most likely among all the planets in all the galaxies in the entire Universe. It is uniquely suited for life because of a quantity of exceptional characteristics that are too numerous to have happened strictly by chance. There is much speculation that life exists not only on other planets in the Universe, but also within our Solar System as well. To this day; however, Earth is the only planet in our Solar System, or anywhere else in the Universe, on which life has been proven to exist.

Any planet orbiting a star outside our Solar System would be far too dim to be seen by us even with a telescope because they can only be observed indirectly by their reflected starlight. Scientists recently claim that they have discovered an overwhelming number of "Earthlike" planets in the Milky Way Galaxy, but these claims do not stand up under close scrutiny. Just being the right size at the right distance from the star they are orbiting is far from adequate to render them "Earthlike". These so called "Earthlike" planets cannot be seen, even by telescope, but have been revealed by observing them crossing in front of the star that they are orbiting. The minuscule drop in the star's brightness as the planet crosses in front of the star, as observed from Earth, is their only means of determining that there is possibly a planet in orbit around the star. There are numerous other attributes that are necessary for a planet to be "Earth-like" and have any chance at harboring life. No one has ever proved that any of these "Earth-like" planets have all, or even any, of these characteristics. Any reference to these extra-solar planet's features such as water, atmosphere, rotation, temperature, surface color or material composition obtained from spectral analysis are merely fabricated speculation. Often it will be declared that one of these distant newly discovered planets likely contains liquid water and; therefore, a good probability of life. The presence of liquid water or even complex organic molecules; however, are not sufficient to procreate life. Considerably more is required. If you see one of these distant planets depicted on TV, you can be sure it is a computer generated figment of someone's imagination. No one has ever actually seen one!

Recently, NASA scientists claim they have found the most similar planet to Earth ever discovered and designated it "Earth 2.0". They say that this planet orbits its star in the circumstellar habitable zone otherwise known as the "Goldilocks Region"; the potentially habitable region that is just the right distance for liquid water to form. This planet is; however, 1,400 light years from Earth which means that with our present technology going there would require an impossibly long time. Not only that, there are considerably more reasons why this planet is not anything like Earth. They believe that the planet is 60% larger than Earth with five times the mass and a gravitational force at its surface that is twice as great as on Earth. It hasn't been determined whether it has an atmosphere and if so, what it is composed of. They don't know if there is any protection from cosmic radiation, nor has it been verified if water actually exists in liquid form on the surface. No one has actually ever seen this planet; all we have are artist's conceptions.

Even more recently, the big news is the discovery of seven near Earth size exoplanets in orbit around a dwarf star about the size of Jupiter. These pseudo-scientists claim that at least three of these planets are within the Goldilocks region of their star and could have water and be suitable for life as we know it. This is pure speculation without any scientific backup to substantiate their claim. They state that this star system with seven Earth sized planets is only 40 light years away, only a short distance from Earth astronomically speaking. Really! Just how far away is 40 light years? It is over 235 trillion miles away, but our present capabilities allow us to travel considerably less than 50,000 miles per hour in space. If we could somehow increase our speed to one tenth the speed of light, or about 67 million miles per hour, it would still take about 400 years to reach these exoplanets. Does that sound practical? We are seeing this star system as it existed 40 years ago, not today. Just to converse with someone 40 light years away would take 80 years; 40 years for the message to reach the planet and another 40 years to receive a reply, so the person that sent the message would not even likely be alive to receive a reply.

One of the major reasons that the Earth's temperature resides in a range that is uniquely suitable for life as we know it is the Earth's distance from the Sun. If the Earth were only a few million miles closer to the Sun, the surface of the Earth would become considerably warmer. This would bring about a decrease in the area of the planet's ice and reflectivity resulting in an increase in absorption of the Sun's heat. The sea level would rise from the melting of the land based glaciers and would create an increase in the surface area of the oceans. This in turn would contribute further to the temperature rise since sea water absorbs greater amounts of solar radiation than equal land mass areas. The consequence of the increased evaporation of the sea water would result in an additional temperature rise. This is one of the reasons that our sister planet, Venus, that is in an orbit closer to the Sun, has such a high surface temperature and is not suitable for life. The opposite would occur if the Earth were in an orbit only a few million miles more distant from the Sun. More of the Earth's surface would be covered by ice with increased reflectivity of the Sun's heat. There would be less absorption of heat by sea water since the oceans would cover less of the Earth's surface. Since the oceans would be colder, there would be less evaporation of water from the oceans producing less water vapor in the atmosphere. This greater distance from the Sun is one of the reasons why Mars is so cold in comparison to Earth.

Also, the 23-1/2° tilt on its rotational axis that accounts for our four seasons prevents our yearly climatic changes from becoming too extreme. The distance from the Earth to the Sun, approximately 93 million miles, is just right for the surface temperature to remain in a range that allows for large masses of liquid water to exist year round and sustain life (The so called "Goldilocks Region"). The Earth revolves around the Sun in a slightly elliptical orbit at a speed of approximately 67,000 miles per hour. If the Earth travelled much faster or slower in its orbit around the Sun, its orbit would change from its present narrow habitable zone to one less favorable to life. The Earth's sidereal year around the Sun is consistent to over a thousandth of a second. If this were not true, our years and seasons would vary in length. The Earth's rotation affects the length of the days and nights as well as the climate and tides. The Earth rotates on its axis once every 24 hours. Faster or slower rotation would cause daytime and nighttime temperature extremes and negatively affect the tides. The surface area of the continents, the amount covered by heat reflecting masses of ice, and the quantity of water vapor in the atmosphere all affect the degree of incoming and outgoing heat that contribute to this end result. To the best of our knowledge, our planet has a molten and/or solid iron core. This, in combination with the Earth's rotation, produces a magnetic field that dispels harmful radiation from the Sun that is detrimental to most life forms, including mankind.

Our Earth has a single moon of just the right size, mass and distance to stabilize the Earth's rotation and provide us with beneficial periodic tidal flows. If it were much larger or nearer to the earth, huge tides would result that would overflow the low lands on a regular basis. The Moon is precisely the right size and distance from both the Earth and the Sun to allow complete blocking of the view of the Sun from Earth during a complete solar eclipse and also complete blockage of the Moon by the Earth during a complete lunar eclipse. Is this just another incredible coincidence?

Earth is the only known planet with huge bodies of liquid water that are vital for life to exist as we know it. Without it, the Earth would experience far greater temperature variations. Water has the unique property of contracting when cooled only until it reaches 39° Fahrenheit and then expanding until it freezes, allowing any ice that forms in oceans and lakes to stay on the surface so that the majority remains in liquid form beneath the ice regardless of the daily temperature swings.

The mixture of gases in the atmosphere closest to the Earth's surface is ideal for supporting life. A change of only a few percent in the oxygen content or a slight change in the atmospheric pressure would make life on Earth difficult. Our atmosphere causes millions of meteors to burn up before reaching the surface of the Earth. If the atmosphere were much thinner, many more would reach the earth's surface, causing considerably greater death, destruction, and fires everywhere. Our atmosphere contains a thin highly concentrated ozone layer in the upper stratosphere that further protects life below from harmful ultraviolet radiation.

Our nearest neighboring planet, Mars, is significantly different from Earth in many ways that make it impossible to support human life. Mars does not appear to have an iron core and therefore does not have a magnetic field that dispels harmful radiation from the Sun that is detrimental to most life forms, including us. It is also considerably further from the Sun than Earth with a surface temperature that is too low to allow for liquid water or to readily support human life. The smaller diameter of the planet does not allow for a significant atmosphere. Mars' atmosphere is less than one percent of Earth's atmosphere and consists of over 95% carbon dioxide with only trace amounts of oxygen, so animal and plant life as we know it cannot exist. If any life does exist on Mars, it must be biological in nature, but to date none has ever been detected.

There are scientists that believe it is possible that in the future mankind will be able to terraform the planet Mars by changing the surface and climate sufficiently to provide a hospitable environment capable of supporting human life forms. This is pure fantasy for many reasons. Foremost, where are they going to obtain the massive resources necessary to terraform an entire planet the size of Mars and how will they accomplish this working in such an extremely hostile environment? Furthermore, how are they going to establish an atmosphere with adequate oxygen that will not escape into space? The gravity on Mars is not sufficient to capture and hold onto a suitable atmosphere. Additionally, how will they be able to survive outdoors on a planet that does not have a magnetic shield to protect from solar radiation like on Earth? Even if they could find adequate water, how will they prevent it from freezing? The temperatures on Mars are significantly colder than on Earth due to the planet's considerably greater distance from the Sun. Mars is not in the narrow habitable zone know as the "Goldilocks Region" that allows for liquid water to exist naturally or to maintain an environment that is uniquely suited to life as on Earth. Mars' atmosphere is a near vacuum and the gravity on the surface is only about 38% of Earth's. Mars is considerably farther from the Sun and receives half the light as Earth resulting in equatorial regions with average daytime temperatures similar to Antarctica's interior but experiencing far colder nighttime temperatures. Mars has a more elliptical orbit than Earth, but without its large stabilizing moon that results in extreme seasonal changes. Some theoretical scientists have proposed converting the entire surface of Mars into greenhouses to establish an oxygen rich atmosphere. This is total nonsense; even though Mars is the second smallest planet in the Solar system, the surface area of Mars is still about 56 million square miles. These theoretical astrophysicists believe that it is possible to terraform Mars, but that it would take up to 100,000 years to do so. Even if it was possible, does that sound like a practical undertaking?

Our next nearest neighbor, Venus is about 67 million miles from the Sun and is the closest in size to Earth and similar in terms of mass, density and composition, but it is a very hostile place to live. It has an atmosphere, but it is highly corrosive, consisting of 96% carbon dioxide with only trace amounts of oxygen. Its atmosphere consists of a thick cloud cover that is 92 times denser than the Earth's resulting in an air pressure at the surface that is in excess of 90 times that found on Earth. The surface temperature is between 800 and 950° Fahrenheit, which is hot enough to melt lead and inherently makes it too hot to support human life. There is no evidence of water on Venus; it rains sulfuric acid from its upper clouds and it has no magnetic field. Venus is in retrograde rotation and takes 5,832 Earth hours (243 Earth days) to complete one rotation on its axis; it is the slowest spinning planet in the Solar system with one day on Venus longer than the time required for it to orbit the Sun so the Sun only rises twice in a Venusian year. This is a forbidding planet that is not habitable by humans or probably any other life form as well.

Mercury is too close to the Sun to sustain life because of the extreme radiation it receives and since it too does not have an atmosphere. Mercury is the smallest planet in our Solar System and rotates around the Sun in an exaggerated elliptical orbit. Its rotation around the sun, or year, takes just under 88 Earth-days while one rotation on its axis takes just under 57 days which means that a single day on Mercury is equivalent to about 0.65 Earth-years. It was originally thought that the planet Mercury was tidal locked like our moon, where its orbital period matches its rotational period. This is also known as "captured rotation" where one side constantly faces the Sun and is always exceedingly hot, while the other side always faces away from the Sun and remains extremely cold. This would leave a small zone with temperatures that may be favorable to maintain life if it wasn't for all the other factors that make life impossible on this planet. Doppler radar observation in 1965 proved "captured rotation" of the planet Mercury to be incorrect. In actuality, since Mercury rotates on its axis three times every two years it means that all locations on the planet experience extremes of hot and cold as well as excessive radiation from the sun. This renders it impossible to establish a permanent base of operation anywhere on the planet that would be suitable for sustained human habitation for scientific research even if the remaining harsh obstacles could be overcome.

The four outer planets, Saturn, Jupiter, Uranus and Neptune, are gas giants that are not suitable for life as we know it. Also, they are so far from the Sun that with our present technology we are unable to send anyone there for even a short time to observe them close up.

The planet Jupiter is so large, with such a large gravitational force and located in the correct proximity to our planet that it protects the Earth from impact from many large meteors that are in the vicinity and would otherwise be likely to strike Earth. Is it reasonable to assume that all these unique characteristics of our Earth and Solar System came about strictly by chance as many scientists claim? It is extremely unlikely!

Another wildly accepted theory by astrophysicists is that life came to Earth on asteroids or comets from outer space; or if not life per-se, at least the building blocks necessary for the creation of life. This makes no sense at all! Where did this life or DNA originate, how did it manage to escape its planet's gravity and hitch a ride on an asteroid or comet, and how far or long did it have to travel in totally unsuitable conditions not conducive to life as we know it to get here? If life did arrive on Earth from somewhere in outer space, it must have been able to survive and prosper on the surface of our planet in a sterile environment since at that time there was nothing available on Earth capable of supporting life. Isn't it considerably more likely that life originated on Earth itself since, as far as we know, Earth is the most uniquely suited planet in the known Universe for life to flourish?

When you read about astronomers detecting planets deep in space that are similar to Earth and may be capable of supporting life, they are not revealing the full implications of their discovery. They are only able to detect anything possibly resembling a planet by measuring a nearly indiscernible drop (less than 1%) in the starlight when the object passes in front of the star it orbits. They have never actually observed anything outside our solar system that even resembles a planet. Everything that is revealed to the public is faked or an artist's rendition of what they believe is out there. Furthermore, they are not looking at the entire picture when they make these ludicrous claims. They believe that because this planet orbits at the preferred "goldilocks" distance from its parent star to possibly contain liquid water or for some other simple rationale that might allow it to support and sustain life they don't even consider any of the myriad of other requirements for life to exist as we know it on Earth. They just assume on the basis of the planet having one or a few of the multitude of necessities to support life that it is Earth-like. This is not rational thinking and does not epitomize the scientific method.

9

EVOLUTION VERSUS CREATIONISM

The belief that science is the only true source of human intellect and that the Universe is strictly godless and materialistic is what is known as scientism. It is in itself unscientific in that it embraces dogmatic beliefs that cannot be confirmed by science alone. For some unknown reason, many scientists, mathematicians and engineers choose not to consider recorded history in their scientific endeavors even though the concept of science is relatively new. They prefer to start from scratch with only concocted theories as their starting point and then attempt to make these illogical assumptions work to arrive at their predetermined conclusion. Maybe, if they paid more attention to what has been recorded in the past, their theories would bear greater credibility and they would not have to rely on manipulating the facts to arrive at their desired conclusion.

Many uphold a belief in evolution and adamantly denounce creationism as religion without merit. These people are only fooling themselves! A belief in the "Big Bang Theory" is not science, but an unfounded belief in an atheistic form of creationism that must be accepted on faith alone. In order for the "Big Bang" to have occurred, all the known laws of physics must be repealed at the moment that their imaginary singularity erupted into the birth of the Universe. Otherwise, if it was infinitely denser than any black hole as they propose, it would have instantly collapsed back into itself since, as their hypothesis implies, nothing could escape, including light. This is their own statement; black holes, although there may be such a thing, are just another theory. They have only been theorized mathematically; they have never been proven to even exist. That is why they had to create the idea of "Cosmic Inflation" and temporarily repeal the known laws of physics. They cannot explain where this singularity came from or what caused this explosion of infinitely dense and hot matter to create the beginning of the entire Universe and time. Furthermore, if in the beginning there was no space, time, matter or motion, how were they created if not by an irrefutably superior intellectual identity? If the Universe was created this way, and it is doubtful, it must have been created by intelligent design unless you believe in magic! They claim that the Universe is nearly 14 billion years old and that all space and matter is expanding into an emptiness that is devoid of space or time. Obviously, this is only an assumption that can never be proven. If the Universe is expanding as proposed by the "Big Bang Theory", what is it expanding into; what exists outside the expanding Universe? Moreover, if the Universe is expanding, what caused the gasses that were ejected at the moment of the Big Bang to contract, rotate and form individual stars? They don't have a credible explanation for any of this; they expect us to accept it on faith alone.

Evolutionists come up with all kinds of illogical theories as to what existed before the "Big Bang". Speculation of an infinite number of universes where every possible outcome is happening simultaneously is one. That takes quite an imagination! Another suggestion is that there are an infinite number of dimensions that have always existed. They also fail to mention where they came from or where they are now. Or, maybe there are only ten dimensions; this is something that has been proposed based on supposedly advanced mathematical equations in string theory. Speculation on these outlandish propositions is not a problem as long as they are not taken too seriously as they can never be verified.

Although evolutionists claim that humans have been on Earth for over a million years, written historic records concur with the Biblical explanation and only go back a few thousand years. There are fossils of dinosaurs and other plants and mammals that may have existed prior to man, but there is no historical account of man's prehistoric existence and no evidence of human civilization prior to about 4000 BC. Even though the Bible is not a scientific book per se, there are numerous instances where Biblical statements portend scientific discoveries that have been proven to be technically correct.

Judaism, Christianity and Islamic religions all acknowledge that the Old Testament is the word of the same God. The Old Testament was written around 1,200 to 100 BC and the New Testament in all probability around 50 to 100 AD. The Quran was not written until considerably later at the beginning of the seventh century AD. The premise that these documents were "inspired by God" does not mean that these words were written by God. With the difficulty in copying manuscripts and creating books during that period of time, it would be a monumental task to perpetuate a hoax of this magnitude. It would be quite a coincidence to believe that the Bible was a work of fiction and everyone was wrong in their beliefs. This is exactly what advocates of evolution would have you believe.

There is more than one version of the Bible and other religious documents due to a number of factors. One of these is due to different translations of the original manuscripts into various other languages. The Old Testament was mostly written in

Hebrew with a few chapters written in Aramaic and the New Testament was written in Greek. These are often translated again into other languages and more substance is lost in these subsequent translations. Another problem arises from heads of different churches or religious organizations modifying the original manuscripts or disregarding some of the documents to more closely align with their religious dogmas and interpretations. Regardless of the somewhat different versions of these documents, the universal premise remains the same; the historical evidence overwhelming confirms that life was not created by chance alone.

The simplest cell requires several hundred proteins and DNA code. DNA is the densest information storage system ever created and consists of extremely large complex molecules that contain the blueprint for all life. The DNA molecule is so complex that the information stored in one human DNA molecule contains enough data to fill a million-page encyclopedia, or about 1,000 books. Bio-engineers have recently been able to store around 700 terabytes (700 trillion bytes) of information in a single gram of DNA, smashing the previous DNA data density record by a thousand times. The DNA from a single human cell contains all the information in a complex language code necessary to design and construct a complete human being with over 100 trillion cells. No amount of evolution through the trial-and-error process of natural selection could bring into being anything this complex over any period of time, even tens or hundreds of billions of years. The DNA code is self-replicating and self-correcting with information that could only have been created through intelligent design. Can anyone explain how this could happen purely by chance regardless of the time available? If the simplest life form cannot materialize by chance alone, there is a much greater probability that life was created by a far superior intelligence than man has ever possessed.

Science has only been in existence for a relatively short period of time, and has not proven anything outside the narrow confines of our everyday worldly events. Religion and the belief in a superior intelligence have a many thousand year history to lend credibility to its claims. Besides history, what other phenomena, if any, provide credence to the likelihood that there is a supreme being that created the Universe and that it didn't just materialize from nothing? What about the scientific evidence that supports near death experiences (NDEs) and an afterlife? In most instances, these NDEs are not verifiable and cannot be proven to be veridical by skeptics if they consider death by its strictest definition to be irreversible. In a few instances; however, the information that is acquired are verifiable events that could not have been obtained in any other way, such as events that were witnessed occurring in an adjacent room or even a significant distance from the person's comatose body. There are literally thousands of cases of near death experiences (NDEs) witnessed over a period of thousands of years that seem to provide a glimpse of an afterlife in a spirit world. These accounts of NDEs, for the most part, have many characteristics in common. NDEs are eerily similar in that most consist of a perceived passage into a different realm, usually through a tunnel towards a bright light, meeting up with relatives that had passed away or with a superior being. There have been a number of cases documented where the blind have been able to see during out-of-body experiences. In a few cases even those that were blind from birth and did not have any perception of what vision was experienced sight during their NDE, but were still blind when they returned to life in their material bodies. Even very young children have described events during NDEs that they could not have obtained from their worldly experiences. In many cases the person experiencing the NDE states that they were able to pass through solid objects as if they weren't there.

This is not as far-fetched as it may seem since in reality solid objects have been proven to be an illusion. All matter consists of atoms made up of even smaller components held together by strong nuclear forces, but composed mainly of empty space. If the human spirit exists in separate dimensions that are not affected by the forces in our known three-dimensional Universe, this is a definite possibility. It is known that extremely small sub-atomic particles pass through the spaces between solid mater all the time. This is one of the reasons why it is so difficult to get these particles to collide in a particle accelerator.

The majority of people that believe that there is no God or afterlife suggest that only science matters, because their beliefs can be proven through science and religion cannot. Nonsense! Belief in a supreme being has thousands of years of history on its side; science does not. Not only has science only been around for a short period of recorded history, but it proves nothing since there is an inconsistency between macro scale physics and micro scale quantum mechanics. They do not agree. Additionally, humans have not advanced to the point where they can unequivocally state that they have grasped even a fraction of all the knowledge available. We are still in the dark ages in many of our scientific endeavors. Very little is known about the properties of our Universe. For instance our best attempt to date to create a craft capable of interstellar travel consists of chemical reaction rockets that have been around for centuries. This method of propulsion is crude and inefficient and will never result in deep space travel. Also, we are only capable of crashing sub-atomic particles together on a extremely small scale using enormously large and expensive equipment in a futile attempt to discover additional information on our microcosm; and then only with very limited success. The findings obtained from these rudimentary experiments are not scientific, but only result in conjecture subject to considerable interpretation.

From all that humans on Earth can surmise we live in a three-dimensional world consisting of three spatial dimensions; those of length, height and depth (x, y & z axes) with possibly a fourth temporal dimension of time that we can perceive, but are unable to measure directly or entirely understand. Are there more dimensions that we are unaware of and cannot comprehend? Maybe! To try to understand the concept of additional dimensions, imagine a universe with only two dimensions, those of length and height. We encounter similar examples on a daily basis such as a flat TV screen, a computer monitor, an I-pad or a cell phone screen. Although not actually two-dimensional, these analogies are two-dimensional for all practical purposes and serve adequately to help us understand this concept. Try to imagine a person that lives in this two-dimensional universe. His entire existence would consist of only length and height without any concept of a third dimension, depth. For example when you view a TV screen from your three-dimensional perspective, you see only length and height. Depth is represented on the two-dimensional screen by objects getting larger and smaller, since true depth perception does not exist in a two-dimensional universe. The person living in this two-dimensional universe could not observe the third dimension that we live in and could never see anyone or anything in it even though it exists. Now try to imagine someone like us that lives in and is aware of only a three-dimensional spatial universe. What if there is a fourth spatial dimension or even more? From our known three-dimensional existence, we cannot observe anyone or anything outside our known sphere of reality even though it may exist. Does this concept seem out of the realm of believability? Is it any more improbable than the unconfirmed "Big Bang Theory" that requires creation of the entire Universe from nothing (an immensely dense and hot singularity), the initial repeal of all the known laws of physics (to make the predetermined mathematical equations work), the creation of dark matter (required to explain why the Universe appears to contain much more matter than can be accounted for in our visible stars) and dark energy (required to explain the unsubstantiated expansion of the Universe)? Or is it any more implausible than "Darwinian Evolution" that requires the spontaneous creation of all life from nothing but organic and inorganic chemicals in a sterile environment, and the progression from single-celled creatures without inherent intellect to mankind itself without any outside influence or intelligent involvement?

Also, what about the significance of time; is it real or just a figment of our imagination? We can't detect it with any of our senses and we only exist in the present, not in the future or the past. According to Einstein's hypothesis, as one approaches the speed of light, time slows down until it stops when the speed of light is reached. Maybe in the fourth or additional dimensions time as we know it ceases to exist and all matter is converted into pure energy. This would account for a number of things that support both evolutionist and creationist hypotheses. For instance, sightings of UFOs that cannot be satisfactorily explained, the creation of extraordinarily complex crop circles in an implausibly short time frame, hypothetical sightings of extraterrestrial beings and ghosts, the existence of "Heaven" outside our perception of reality, the NDEs proclamation of traveling through a tunnel towards a bright light and reuniting with those who have previously departed, the purported observance of religious entities, alleged miracles and other unidentified phenomenon.

The Earth and presumably the entire Universe is in reality far different than is observed or can be imagined by most. No object and no one have ever actually touched anything else. Even all the atoms of our very own bodies do not touch. Everything consists of subatomic particles held in close proximity to each other by strong nuclear forces. The only time contact may possibly occur is in nuclear fusion reactions when atoms fuse together with serious repercussions. No matter how different things appear, everything is made up of the same basic material. All that can be observed by man on Earth with the naked unaided eye is in reality an illusion. This alleged scientific idea that all creation began exclusive of any assistance from a superior intelligence is something that has been devised by man relatively recently in history. Those that perpetuate these ideas to discredit religious beliefs do so exclusive of any historic backing or credibility. They are extremely naïve and/or arrogant if they suppose for one moment that they know without reservation that whatever they believe is unquestionably true. Not only does history validate the perception of creation by a superior intelligence, but science overwhelming corroborates the same inference.

10

CONCLUSIONS

The majority of the people living on Earth today are not scientists and do not have the substantial technical background essential in understanding why it is virtually impossible for the Universe and life itself to have evolved from nothing. Most of those that believe in evolution today accept it on faith alone based on what they are being taught by whom they trust as knowledgeable scientists or from what they have been taught in school or have heard through other trusted media. Most people today cannot comprehend the complexity of the Universe or even that of the simplest life forms on planet Earth, much less humans or the micro-universe. Nor can they comprehend the vast distances that the Cosmos encompass' or how small things can be. For example, even the short distance, in terms of not only the Universe but even just our own Milky Way Galaxy, to our nearest star system Alpha Centauri is incomprehensibly far at over 25,000,000,000,000 (25 trillion) miles. In comparison, a bacterium is only 0.00000001 (one hundred-millionth) meter long with other subatomic particles such as electrons or quarks considerably smaller yet. These extreme magnitudes are so remote from what is experienced in everyday life that they cannot be fully comprehended by anyone. For this reason, many are led to believe that the media is providing them with facts, without using common sense to question the validity of their statements. It appears that "common sense" today is not at all that common!

There are many new categories of pseudo-scientists that come with terms such as "theoretical", "astro", "cosmo" or "evolutionary" that do not deal with real science at all or only with conjecture, such as Theoretical Physicist, Theoretical Biologist, Astrophysicist, Cosmologist or Evolutionary Biologist. Anything that deals with theory is just a supposition, assumption or hypothesis and does not qualify as real science until it is proven to be true beyond all reasonable doubt. It is not science unless it is something that was observed by the one proposing the theory and that appears to be a valid explanation of a phenomenon that is supported by observation, experimentation and reasoning. Regrettably, many of these theories, such as the Big Bang Theory, the Darwinian Theory of Evolution and the Expanding Universe Theory are now considered by the majority of not only scientists but the main stream public as well to be fact without confirmation. Many of the more recent explanations of unidentified phenomenon are made based on these unproven original theories and lead to increased erroneous conclusions. Very few appear to be questioning the validity of the original assumptions as they should be due to the numerous errors, unproven hypotheses and outright lies that many are based upon. It must be remembered that the earlier scientists that declared that the Earth was flat or that the Earth was the center of the Universe were also highly regarded in their day. Although their assumptions were deemed to be accurate at the time, they were all proven to be incorrect at a later date. Who is to say that these renowned scientists of today will not also have their theories proven incorrect in the future? It appears very likely that an appreciable percentage will!

All evidence indicates that life on Earth was created through intelligent design, and not by chance. Although most of the seven billion plus people that live on Earth today believe in some kind of religion, it does not even have to be taken into consideration to disprove the validity of evolution. Evolution is not science, but the theory of creation for the religion of atheism. This is why so many people that believe in evolution take offense when their unfounded beliefs are challenged and why they are not interested in listening to other points of view. It takes considerably more faith to believe in evolution than it does to believe in intelligent design and all scientific evidence points towards this conclusion.

These scientists need to take the time to prove or disprove these theories that are without scientific foundation first before accepting them as fact when indeed they are not. They also need to rethink their original hypotheses when the experimentation and observations do not agree instead of modifying their results to agree with the original theories. Today this is not being done enough. Many have become lazy or arrogant and abandoned the scientific method in favor of voting on a particular theory and then claiming it to be reality with little regard for fact. The majority of the Earth's population, including the intelligent minority, follows the crowd and aligns with the more popular or politically correct view regardless of what nonsense they are being told. Most people today do not take the time to inquire as to the truth or validity of a claim before arriving at a conclusion. Instead, they choose to make their decisions without forethought. You can't assume someone has postulated a correct theory just because he has an advanced degree or a high IQ. A theory can only be proven to be reasonably true to the best of one's knowledge by rigorous observation, experimentation and reasoning. Consensus by a select group of individual scientists, regardless of their credentials, or even a majority vote does not prove anything and is totally in conflict with the scientific method. This is junk science that is being accepted by alleged scientists and perpetuated worldwide by uninformed politicians, the media and educators. Anyone that attempts to go against their agenda are criticized and belittled. The majority of people, with or without advanced degrees and/or high IQs, base their judgment concerning a particular hypothesis not on a thorough evaluation of the entire premise for the original theory, but only on a few, or in many cases only on a single detail. Most people make decisions concerning other countries politics, religion, or ethnicity based on biased opinions without doing research on alternate views even though the majority of people on Earth do not have a passport and have never been to another country outside their country of birth. Governments and the media play a large role in establishing and perpetuating these erroneous opinions. First there was a great apprehension about acid rain and then came the panic over the depletion of the ozone layer. Now it appears that the greatest fear of the day is the overheating of the planet from global warming instigated by the burning of fossil fuels by mankind. None of these so called catastrophes have been shown to amount to anything sufficient to require immediate action to prevent an imminent worldwide disaster.

Another more recent event that is taking place that further adds to the junk science being propagated are the highly paid Hollywood actors or prominent athlete activists that are getting involved in areas where they have absolutely no knowledge on the subject matter. They take a stand on subjects such as global climate change or properties of the Universe based on their flawed beliefs and make alleged documentaries aimed at convincing the public that their erroneous convictions are true and factual. These are people with little or no scientific background, only poorly researched opinions. Unfortunately, there are far too many people today that idolize these false prophets and believe for some unknown reason that because they are movie stars or esteemed athletes that they have superior knowledge in other areas outside their chosen profession. More often than not, they don't!

Today much so-called science is based on what many mostly "theoretical" physicists, mathematicians, astronomers, politicians and scholars "think" or "believe" to be true, not on actual facts. Can 97% of these "scientists" be wrong on a particular subject; even a major one? Absolutely! The number of people that believe in something does not have any direct correlation with its validity. For example, during the time of Nicolaus Copernicus, how many people believed that the Earth was at the center of the Universe? In all likelihood it was the majority, and they were all wrong; the same holds true today. Unfortunately many people, even those with advanced degrees or high IQ's, actually believe these fabrications without actually taking the time to question their validity before coming to a conclusion. Believing in something does not make it true no matter how convinced one is that their assumption holds merit. Unfortunately many myths are being perpetuated today because of this abandonment of the scientific method in favor of reliance on poorly researched conclusions without justification.

It is unfortunate that so many people in positions of authority or influence are so set on economic or political gain, or fame as to lie or deliberately mislead others into believing falsehoods to satisfy their own personal arrogance or greed. Until these dishonest scientists, mathematicians, educators, politicians and media choose to tell the truth, the majority of people on Earth will be duped into believing these deceptions. Regrettably, this will in all probability not come to pass anytime soon since the majority of politicians, media and teachers worldwide continue to perpetuate these myths.

REFERENCES

Top Ten Scientific Facts Proving Charles Darwin's Theory of Evolution is Wrong, False, and Impossible
Bible Life Ministries, Kent R. Rieske, Boulder, CO

Debunking Evolution: Problems Between the Theory and Reality, the False Theory of Evolution
New Geology US, 2006-2016 John Michael Fischer

The Top Ten
Man's Greatest Achievements – Top Ten List
www.thetopten.com/mans-achievements

BBC Future, How Fast Could Humans Travel Safely Through Space
By Adam Hadhazy, August 10, 2015

Where does "Prehistoric Man" Fit into the Bible's History?
Creation Moments Radio Scripts 2006

Piltdown Man from Wikipedia, the Free Encyclopedia

The "Big Bang" is Just Religion Disguised as Science
What really happened Com LLC
Michael Rivero 1994-2016

The Big Bang Theory – A Flawed Concept
Physics myths org . uk
Thomas Smid (M.Sc. Physics, Ph.D. Astronomy)

The Top Ten Problems with the Big Bang
Apeiron, Vol. 9, No. 2, April 2002

Taking Back Astronomy, Chapter 3
The Age of the Universe, Part1
Dr. Jason Lisle, March 13, 2008

The Bible, the Quran, and Science
Dr. Maurice Bucaille
The Holy Scriptures Examined in the Light of Modern Knowledge
Translated from French by Alastair D. Pannell and the Author

The Lahore Ahmadiyya Movement in Islam
English Translation of the Holy Quran
Maulana Muhammad Ali, 1999-2012

Prove Evolution is False – Even without the Bible
Mario Seiglie, Jan 7, 2012

Eggshell from Wikipedia, the Free Encyclopedia

Fossils – Facts – and – Finds.com
The Cambrian Period: An Explosion of Life, 2005-2013

How Fossils Work – Bone to Stone: Building Fossils
Tracy V. Wilson

Fossilization – How Fossils Form

CO_2 Nears 400 ppm – Relax! It's Not Global Warming 'End Times' – But Only a 'Big Yawn' – Climate Depot Special Report
Marc Morano – Human Events, May 14, 2013

Principia Scientific International
The Four Known Scientific Ways Carbon Dioxide Cools Earth's Climate
Dr. Pierre Latour PE, August 22, 2014

An Inconvenient Truth - A Global Warning
Global Warming Documentary by Al Gore
Paramount Pictures DVD Video
Copyright 2006 by Participant Productions
& Book: An Inconvenient Truth – The Planetary Emergency of Global Warming and What We Can Do About It
Published by Rodale, Produced by Melcher Media
Copyright 2006 by Al Gore

Radiometric Dating: Problems with the Assumptions – Answers in Genesis
Andrew A. Snelling, August 04, 2010

The Dating of the New Testament – bethinking.org
Norman Geisler, 2007

In What Language was the Bible First Written?
Biblica, The International Bible Society

Biblical Evidence for Long Creation Days
Rich Deem, Sept. 21, 2007

God of Wonders, DVD
Exploring the Wonders of Creation, Conscience, and the Glory of God
Eternal Publications, 2008

How the First Plants Came to Be, Scientific America
David Biello, February 16, 2012

The Origin of Plants, Answers in Genesis
Roger Patterson, April 5, 2007

Detonation Velocity – Wikipedia
Explosive Material, New World Encyclopedia
October 11, 2013

The Origin of Species by means of Natural Selection or, the Preservation
of Favored Races in the Struggle for Life
Charles Darwin, November 22, 1859
Published by John Murray, Publishers of London

Darwin's Ghost
The Origin of Species Updated
Steve Jones, Copyright 2000

Climate Realists
Climate Change – the Real Cause
By Geoff Duffy, PhD
Professor of Chemical Engineering

Dark Winter or, How the Sun is Causing a 30-year Cold Spell
John L. Casey, Copyright 2014
Printed in U.S. and U.K. by Humanix Books

Institute for Energy Research (IER)
News Flash: Wind Power is Not Cheaper than Coal (Latest Analysis)
By Travis Fisher, May 23, 2016

Astronomy Essentials
How Earth Looks from Outer Space
By Deborah Byrd, August 29, 2016

If the Universe is 13.8 Billion Years Old, How Can We See 46 Billion
Light Years Away?
http://medium.com
Ethan Siegel, March 2, 2018

Report 1235, Standard Atmospheric – Tables and Data for Altitudes
to 65,800 Feet
International Civil Aviation Organization - Montreal, Canada &
Langley Aeronautical Laboratory - Langley Field, Va.
National Advisory Committee for Aeronautics, March 3, 1915

www.quora.com (2017)
Does Methane Burn or Explode

Science Daily, November 15, 2007
What Determines Sky's Colors at Sunrise and Sunset?
University of Wisconsin – Madison

www.complex.com, February 20, 2015
So, What Exactly Is the Illuminati Conspiracy?
By Jason Duaine Hahn

NBC News – Science, May 22, 2014
Conspiracy Theories Abound as U.S. Military Closes HAARP

The New York Times,
The Negative Social Impact of Conspiracy Theories
Karen Douglas, January 04, 2016

Chemical & Engineering News, November 07, 2016
Cold Fusion Died 25 Years Ago, but the Research Lives On
By Stephen K. Ritter

Myles Power, February 02, 2017
A Review of Dr. Judy Wood's Book "Where Did the Towers go? –
Where Did the Buildings go?

Geophysical Institute,
University of Alaska, Fairbanks
HAARP Antenna Design

Popular Science
Bodies in Motion: Exploring the Human Limits of Future Travel
www.answers.yahoo.com
Jacob Ward – May 16, 2011

Inconvenient Facts
The science that Al Gore doesn't want you to know
Gregory Wrightstone, 2017
Silver Crown Productions, LLC

ABOUT THE AUTHOR

I am a retired mechanical engineer and first time author. My qualifications to write a technical book with credibility that requires a scientific background consists of a BSME (Bachelor of Science in Mechanical Engineering) degree from a fully accredited major university and over 30 years of application and design engineering experience with additional university studies in meteorology and electronics. A Bachelor of Science in Mechanical Engineering is a discipline that applies the principles of engineering, physics and material science that requires significant scientific study and comprension of the scientific method. It requires an understanding of core concepts that include mechanics, kinematics, thermodynamics, material science, structural analysis, chemistry, electronics and mathematics (primarily linear algebra, calculus and differential equations). All mechanical engineers with a Bachelor of Science degree have a minor in mathematics. Mechanical engineering is the broadest and most diverse of all engineering disciplines. A mechanical engineer uses applied science with the objective toward practical utility as opposed to theoretical scientists that are usually concerned with scientific hypotheses and abstract mathematics and spend considerable time in the laboratory attempting to understand scientific principles and refine existing theories.